World Minorities in the Eighties

A Third Volume in the Series

edited by
Georgina Ashworth
formerly Research Director, Minority Rights Group

Quartermaine House Ltd.
Windmill Road, Sunbury, Middx., U.K.
1980

First published by Quartermaine House Ltd. 1980
© Quartermaine House Ltd. and Minority Rights Group
ISBN 0 905898 11 7

*Companion to this book "World Minorities" Volumes 1 & 2 edited by
Georgina Ashworth, published by Quartermaine House*

Printed in Great Britain
by Unwin Brothers Limited, Old Woking, Surrey

Contents

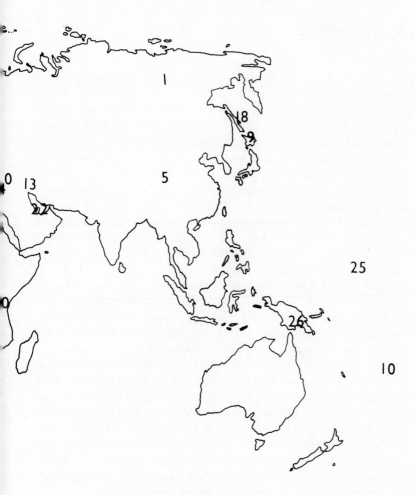

The figures on the map refer to the Chapter numbers

Introduction

It is always heart-breaking to see people of talent and goodwill being sapped and destroyed by a system not of their own making but to which they were prepared to commit themselves from a belief in promises bogusly given. This may be said of both individuals and groups, of institutions and constitutions. It is also a real and philosophical tragedy that a group (or an individual) will only be counted as a political and social entity when conflict of some form has been recorded. Conditions that engender conflict are condemned only in retrospect, often when they are too late to repair. Those whose natures and societies are peaceable will suffer more deeply, for they will respond without aggression very much longer — by absorbing the fears and threatening perceptions into what becomes a "nearly bottomless well of self-depreciation". They are really, like the extinct Tasmanians who did not "stand up and fight", theoretically the truly civilised.

History in the Western tradition is computed from bogus promises and broken treaties: it is a chart of sacrifice. There is little record of anticipation or prevention, and even conciliation comes after heart-break and destruction. It is also essentially androcentric in that heroism of the visible sacrifice is more creditable than the quietist social withdrawal. Domination survives off the unrecorded subordination of the dispossessed rather than through victories on battlefields. The most valuable political evolution of the twentieth century would be a culturally and politically neutral, non-strategic, entity that prevents, by anticipation and conciliation, the outbreak of conflict and pre-empts necessary sacrifice. Inexorably looking into what already exists, the UN system, we find that for minorities there is a Subcommission for the Protection of Minorities and Prevention of Discrimination. But it neither prevents nor protects, being obsessed with rather grander gestures. The small, social — slightly scorned — bodies like the Status of Women Commission are where hopes should be placed. There, centuries-old problems are being dusted and re-examined, and a new understanding of human society may evolve.

This volume is the third collection of papers on the fates and diversities of minorities contributed by volunteers of many interests and occupations. Each paper may be read on its own, or as a chapter among many purveying different aspects of human activity and suffering. So can each volume, and the preface to each volume. This one is dedicated to all those — the world over — who have given me help and support during my five years' work for the Minority Rights Group, and whose friendship I continue to treasure. Their names are too numerous to list, but they will recognise themselves in this paragraph. In particular, I must thank Pat Oakley, Jackie Johnson (now Thorpe) and Georgina Relly without whom this book would not be in the reader's hands.

Georgina Ashworth
London, January 1980

Since the completion of several of these chapters, some of the events predicted have taken place. There have been developments in Chad, Iran, Israel, the Pacific Islands and Liberia in particular. Nevertheless, I feel the political sensitivity and acumen of the authors should be recognised in retaining these chapters as they are, forming the background to these changing events.

Georgina Ashworth
June 1980

Preface

Minority Rights, Autonomy and Power-Sharing

Arendt Lijphart

Minorities of all kinds — cultural, religious, linguistic, ethnic, and racial — are ubiquitous in today's world. Almost all states have one or more minority groups within their national territories, and minorities frequently live on different sides of state borders. Consequently, the treatment of minorities presents a moral and political problem with both domestic and international ramifications. It is of vital importance that both statesmen and citizens pay more attention to this question — a major educational task to which the Minority Rights Group has made an outstanding contribution. In addition, it is imperative that we think of practical solutions to minority problems which are fair both to the minorities and to the societies of which they form a part. I shall devote this preface to the latter subject.

My comparative research into the viability of democracy in divided, or plural, societies has led me to the conclusion that the ideal solution to the problem of minorities is the establishment of a type of democracy which I have labeled "consociational democracy," using a term originated by the 17th century political theorist Johannes Althusius. I started this line of research with a study of democratic practices and institutions in the inhospitable environment of the religiously and ideologically divided society of the Netherlands (*The Politics of Accommodation: Pluralism and Democracy in the Netherlands*). My next step was to extend the analysis to similar European and non-Western countries, such as Belgium, Switzerland, Austria, Lebanon, and Malaysia (see my *Democracy in Plural Societies: A Comparative Exploration*). In these books, my main concern is the stability and effectiveness of democracy in societies with a low degree of homogeneity and consensus rather than the problems of minorities as such. However, the two subjects overlap to a considerable extent, and I believe that consociational theory contains many ideas that have a direct practical relevance for the treatment of minorities. In order to demonstrate this point, I shall first discuss the principal characteristics of consociational democracy and emphasise not only the contrast between the consociational and the better-known majoritarian types of democracy but also the close connection between consociationalism and widely accepted principles of justice and fairness. Second, I shall argue that if for any reason a democratic system cannot be established or maintained in a country, the non-democratic regime that is optimal for the treatment of minorities is a "consociational oligarchy." Finally, I shall discuss to what extent consociational principles may be applied when a minority is so small that it is either impractical or unacceptable to the majority or other larger minorities that its rights and interests are accommodated by means of a full-fledged consociational regime.

Consociational democracy has four basic characteristics: grand coalition or power-sharing, autonomy, minority veto, and proportionality. Power-sharing and autonomy are the primary principles; the veto and proportionality rules are of secondary but still fundamental importance.

1. Power-sharing or government by grand coalition — I shall use these terms synonymously — means that the political leaders of all significant and clearly identifiable segments of a society cooperate in governing the country. Power-sharing can take several different institutional forms, for instance, grand coalition cabinets in parliamentary systems, "grand" councils or committees with important advisory or coordinating functions, and grand coalitions consisting of the president and other high functionaries in presidential systems. Power-sharing may be contrasted with the government-versus-opposition pattern of majoritarian democracy, exemplified by the Westminster model. Majority rule entails the concentration of political power in the hands of the majority or a coalition of minorities and the exclusion from power of the representatives of the rest of the population.

We have become so accustomed to equating democracy with majority rule that we tend to forget that majority rule is democratic only when there is alternation in office. When a political minority can increase its electoral appeal and become a majority, it can take over executive power. In such a situation, all groups have a chance to be in the government in the long run. But when the dividing lines between majority and minority or between several minorities are fixed rather than fluid, it is likely that one or more minorities will continually lose elections and will be permanently excluded from power. It is widely accepted that the first and foremost meaning of democracy is participation in making decisions. This meaning of democracy is violated when a minority lacks any reasonable chance to take part in the government. In short, majority rule in deeply divided societies is likely to be profoundly undemocratic, and the only democratic system is one that allows participation in government by a coalition of all groups, majority and minority, on a more or less permanent basis.

2. The logical complement of power-sharing is a maximum degree of autonomy for the minority groups. On all issues of common interest, the decisions should be made jointly by the representatives of all groups; on all other matters, decision-making should be left to each separate group. In contrast with majority rule, this autonomy entails minority rule over the minority itself with regard to a specified area of activities that are the minority's exclusive concern.

Although minority autonomy deviates from the principles of majoritarian democracy, it is not at all undemocratic. In particular, the idea of autonomy is widely accepted in federal theory and practice as far as geographically defined minority groups are concerned. The consociational idea of autonomy may be regarded as an extension of the federal concept to all minorities regardless of whether they are territorially concentrated or dispersed.

3. The minority veto also violates majoritarian principles but the idea that minorities should be able to veto any proposal that threatens their basic rights is not at all alien to the democratic tradition either. It is akin to the rule in most democracies that more than a simple majority is required to amend the Constitution or, in other words, that a minority of a certain minimum size can prevent constitutional changes to which it objects.

4. The final consociational principle is proportionality. It serves as the basic standard of political representation, civil service appointments, and allocation of public funds. Again, the contrast with majoritarianism is obvious. On the other hand, it

should be recognised that in majority-rule democracies patterned after the Westminster model, the geographically defined electoral constituencies should be equal — or not too unequal. Proportional representation is the logical extension of this idea to non-territorial groups. Also, the assumption in majoritarian democracies is that non-discrimination will automatically lead to the fair representation of minorities in civil service positions and to the allocation of fair shares of public funds to minorities. In plural societies, genuine non-discrimination is almost impossible to achieve, and proportionality is a more potent guarantee of fairness for minorities.

When we look at actual examples of consociational democracy, we find that they do not possess all of the characteristics of the ideal model described above. Instead, they are approximations of this ideal. It is important to emphasise, however, that consociationalism does not have to be perfect in order to protect minority rights and interests.

The deviation from the consociational ideal that occurs most often is the absence, or the merely weak presence, of the veto rule. There are two reasons for this. One difficulty is that it is difficult to specify to what kinds of decisions the veto should apply. But the main problem is that a minority veto contains the danger that it will be used too frequently and indiscriminately, and that it will bring the entire government to a standstill. It may therefore be argued that the minority veto works best if it is based on an informal agreement rather than on a written guarantee.

Another consociational principle that may not be realised optimally is minority autonomy. A federal or a highly decentralised system offers the best method to achieve autonomy for minorities, but it requires that the minorities be geographically concentrated. If this is not the case, it is still possible to approximate the ideal, for instance, by giving minorities the right to run their own cultural and educational institutions.

An examination of the actual cases of consociational democracy provides many examples of the successful implementation of consociational principles. I cannot discuss these examples in detail in this preface, but let me identify the countries and periods that offer the most useful lessons of how consociationalism can be practiced: Austria during the period of Catholic-Socialist grand coalitions from 1945 to 1966, Belgium since World War

I and, as far as its linguistic communities are concerned, especially since 1970, the Netherlands from 1917 to 1967, Switzerland from 1943 on, Lebanon in the 1943–1975 period, Cyprus during the few years from its independence in 1960 until 1963, Malaysia from 1955 until 1969, Surinam in the 1955–1973 period, and the Netherlands Antilles since 1950. In addition, there are two interesting examples of "semi-consociational" democracy: Israel since its independence in 1948, and Canada — both the contemporary Canadian system and, even more clearly, the pre-democratic United Province of Canada from 1840 to 1867.

Of course, these cases contain lessons not only of the successes of consociationalism but also of some of its failures. These failures must not be exaggerated, however, even when the entire consociational system appears to have failed. In particular, the collapse of the Lebanese system of carefully balancing and accommodating the different Christian and Moslem minorities in the civil war that began in 1975, is frequently cited as proof that in the long run consociationalism "does not work." I firmly believe that such a conclusion is incorrect, and that it entails especially dangerous consequences if it prevents a serious examination of consociational solutions for minority problems.

The main cause of the breakdown of the consociational regime in Lebanon was not so much the inherent weakness of the system as the extraordinary external pressure of the Middle East conflict and the increasingly heavy burden of the presence of large numbers of Palestinian refugees and guerrilla forces on Lebanese soil. To be sure, there were also deep internal disagreements about certain aspects of the consociational system, in particular, the fixed 6:5 ratio that gave the Christians a permanent majority in the legislature in spite of the fact that the Moslems had grown to at least numerical equality with the Christians by the middle of the 1970's. But the way to solve this problem is not to abolish consociationalism but to adopt a more flexible rule of proportionality. Finally, it would be completely unrealistic to expect that in a deeply divided country like Lebanon, majority-rule democracy would work better than consociationalism. In fact, the correct lesson to be learned from the Lebanese tragedy of the late 1970's is that the only hope for a peaceful and democratic solution — short of partition — is not to abandon consociationalism, but to return to a strengthened consociational system.

Full-fledged consociational democracy, or a close approximation, constitutes the optimal solution for the protection of minority rights and interests, but it is not always realistic to try to achieve this goal. Does consociational theory suggest possibilities that fall short of the ideal, but that are nevertheless helpful in protecting minorities as much as possible?

There are two situations in which this question has special relevance. First, the majority of the states in the contemporary world are not ruled democratically, and although some may turn toward democracy in the foreseeable future, most non-democratic countries are likely to remain non-democratic. In these less than ideal circumstances, it may still be possible to apply some of the consociational devices. Second, it may be difficult to accommodate very small minorities in a pure consociational system, because the larger groups will probably regard the complete sharing of power as entailing disproportionate influence for tiny minorities.

I shall discuss the former subject in this section, but I first want to state a disclaimer. I do not endorse the frequently held view that non-democratic forms of government are more appropriate for certain types of societies than democracy. People who hold this opinion usually think of economically under-developed societies that allegedly require a firm government to guide economic growth, and plural societies that have to be transformed into more homogeneous nations. It is impossible to prove in a general way the superiority or inferiority of any type of government for such societies, but we should be careful not to exaggerate the weaknesses of democracy and to ignore the weaknesses of non-democratic regimes. For instance, a democratic government may find it difficult to promote rapid economic growth because it is under popular pressure to divert economic resources into private consumption and welfare benefits, but non-democratic rulers may waste a country's resources in various other ways. Also, non-democratic governments are not necessarily good nation-builders, because nation-building is a slow process and the possibilities of imposing unity are very limited.

However, given the ubiquity of non-democratic regimes, we must ask which type of non-democratic government offers the best protection of minorities. I believe that the answer is a type of regime that may be called "consociational oligarchy," characterised by two consociational elements. One is the idea of power-sharing by the leaders of all groups in the divided society, whether these leaders are the elected representatives of their respective groups or simply belong to and feel a sense of identification with their groups. This means that a collegial oligarchical regime is preferable to a one-man dictatorship, because a single leader in a plural society is almost inevitably more the representative of one particular group than of the society as a whole. Moreover, it means that a broadly based consociational oligarchy is preferable to an oligarchy drawn from one majority or minority group.

Secondly, a non-democratic form of government is not necessarily a centralised system. Therefore, minorities may be able to find protection in a grant of autonomy either on a territorial basis or as cultural groupings with the right to run their own schools and so on. Especially if minority autonomy and power-sharing by minority leaders are present simultaneously, they may reinforce each other and thus guarantee a much more favourable treatment of minorities than other forms of non-democratic government.

A different problem for the application of consociational democracy is the presence of very small minorities. For instance, for a minority of less than 1% of the total population it is difficult to claim a permanent share of executive power; a power-sharing cabinet would become unwieldy if it had to include representatives of such small groups.

However, there are various ways in which shared power can be introduced without full power-sharing at the highest executive level. First, if a small minority is geographically concentrated to some extent, it may constitute a sufficiently large minority at the regional and local levels to participate in power-sharing executives there. Second, at the national level, minority representatives can serve as advisory members of cabinets with the right to participate in cabinet decision-making only on issues that are of special importance to certain minorities and without a formal vote. Third, committees or councils may be set up by cabinets in order to give advice on matters that especially concern minorities, and even minorities of very small size may be given permanent representation on these. Fourth, legislatures are usually large enough to give representation to small minorities without giving them a disproportionately large influence; this may be accomplished by electoral methods that are either highly proportional (for instance, proportional representation in large multi-member constituencies) or that reserve seats for specified groups. Fifth, it is not at all undemocratic to be generous and to grant small minorities a somewhat larger share of representation than to which their numbers would entitle them.

It may also be difficult to institute autonomy for very small minorities, especially when they do not cluster in a small area, but this is certainly not impossible. One interesting model is provided by the Law of Cultural Self-Government for National Minorities that was adopted in Estonia in 1925. It gave any minority larger than 3,000 people the right to claim cultural autonomy. The extremely permissive lower limit of 3,000 is especially noteworthy. These minorities could set up Cultural Councils, elected by the minority members, with the right to legislate in the educational and cultural fields (schools, libraries, theatres, etc.) and to raise taxes. State subsidies for schools were available to the Councils on an equal basis with other Estonian schools. This Estonian experiment provides an intriguing example of how minimal minorities can enjoy a maximum degree of autonomy.

My main conclusion is that the key to the fair treatment of minorities is the combined application of power-sharing and autonomy. The ideal is a democratic regime in which minorities can participate fully in decision-making at all levels and in which they have exclusive power in those areas which can be defined as regarding only their own interests. When this ideal cannot be attained because of political or numerical considerations, the second best solution is to try to approximate power-sharing and minority autonomy as closely as possible.

Arendt Lijphart, now Professor of Political Science at the University of California San Diego, was formerly at the University of Leiden, the Netherlands, and is author of *The Politics of Accommodation: Pluralism and Democracy in the Netherlands* (University of California Press, Berkeley and London 1968; 2nd edit 1975) and *Democracy in Plural Societies: A Comparative Exploration* (Yale University Press, New Haven and London, 1977).

1 Aboriginal Peoples of Siberia

The Yakuts and those aboriginal groups aggregated in the Soviet census as the "Small Peoples of the North" form the core of the aboriginal population of Siberia. The "Small Peoples" include the Khants (formerly Ostyaks), Mansi (Voguls), Nentsy (Samoyeds), Entsy, Nganasans (Tavgi Samoyeds), Sel'kups (Ostyak Samoyeds), Kets (Yenisei Ostyaks), Evenks (Tungus), Dolgans, Evens (Lamut), Negidals, Nanai (Gold), Ul'chi, Udegei, Orochi, Oroks, Nivkhi (Gilyaks), Chukchi, Koryaks, Itel'men (Kamchadals), Yukagirs, Chuventsy, Tofalars, Soyots, Eskimos, Aleuts, and Saami (Lapps). The total population of these peoples, based on an extrapolation of the 1970 census figures modified for observed growth trends, should be approximately 530,000 in 1980. The Yakut are the largest group, with approximately 340,000 in 1980, and the smallest groups, such as the Tofalars and Soyots, will probably number no more than 200-300. The rate of growth of the aboriginal population as a whole over the decade 1970-1980, based on interim statistics, has averaged approximately 20%. Among many groups with apparently static or declining population figures, the pattern has been one of assimilation into other larger and more vital aboriginal groups — e.g., many Evens have joined the Evenk group, many Evenks and Yukagirs the Yakut, etc. Language is a major aspect of ethnic identity in the U.S.S.R. For this reason, it is significant that as of 1970 some 77.61% of these people continued to claim their native language as their first language, and only 55.02% claim a working knowledge of Russian. It is likely that this population group as a whole is relatively stable over the near future, with marginal groups assimilating primarily into other aboriginal groups and, to a lesser extent, into the Russianized Soviet population, and with Yakuts remaining the most vital in a demographic sense.

The earliest recorded aboriginal-Russian contacts were in the 11th century. A series of military expeditions, including that of Yermak in 1581–85, led to the rapid extension of government authority in Siberia, with only some 65 years between Yermak's crossing of the Urals and the first Russian settlement on the Pacific coast at Okhotsk in the 1640s. By the 18th century all of Siberia and its aboriginal peoples were incorporated into the Russian State, with an administrative system based on hierarchical rule by Russian Governors acting through traditional tribal "princes" (clan leaders); the aboriginal population, although dominant in the North, was already outnumbered in the region as a whole by the Russians. Government interference in aboriginal life was minimal so long as tribute in the form of furs and corvee labour, etc., was forthcoming, but punishment for the sporadic acts of resistence was draconian. The relatively small size of aboriginal groups in Siberia (bands of hunters, trappers, pastoralists, and fishermen) and the absence of strong political and military structures among them made them a very minor threat to Russian hegemony from a very early period. The Russians, with little racial antipathy to the Siberians and a real appreciation of their role in the exploitation of Siberian resources (notably fur), tended to adopt relatively paternalistic policies towards them. As early as the 18th century, the Tsars restricted the access of non-aboriginals to certain prime fur trapping territories in Siberia. In 1822, the Native Code proposed to respect the internal autonomy of the aboriginal communities, to protect native trade, and to alleviate exploitation. Like most of such policies, it was often more honoured in the breach than in the main.

By the early 20th century the aboriginal population had been seriously eroded by disease and alcoholism, economic initiative even in the fur trade was firmly in the hands of often unscrupulous Russians who had in many cases reduced the natives to debt peonage, and the influx of Russian population and capital brought about by the increasing emphasis on mineral exploitation of Siberia seemed to doom the aboriginals to cultural, and then biological, extinction. Only the Yakut had produced even the smallest core of a native intelligentsia.

For the most part the aboriginals stood apart from both sides in the Revolution. However, the Bolsheviks, for complex reasons, early evinced a special concern for the Siberians. The Declaration of the Rights of the People of Siberia in 1918 promised "equal" and "free" development of the tribal peoples. The Yakut Autonomous Soviet Socialist Republic was one of the first established, in 1922. In the 1920s a policy of establishing National Districts (*Okrugs*) and smaller National Areas for the aboriginal groups in Siberia for aboriginals in the Russian Federated Soviet Socialist Republic. Aboriginal people are elected to local *soviets* (councils) in these areas, and are recruited for local Communist Party and administrative posts. The top posts, though often largely symbolic, are regularly held by aboriginals. The Soviet government early on made a serious commitment to the extension of education, health care, and economic resources to aboriginal peoples out of proportion to their numbers or economic and political importance. Native preference in local political advancement, admission to universities and other educational and vocational programs, and waivers of military service (at least prior to World War II) have even led to feelings of resentment among some Russians. Most aboriginals are employed in modern versions of traditional occupations — reindeer husbandry, fishing, fur farming. According to 1970 statistics, less than 1 of the industrial labour force was aboriginal. Natives share in the special pay bonuses for those in arctic hardship areas. Policies towards Siberians have generally been significantly more tolerant than those applied to the larger minorities, even during the collectivisation period when the aboriginals resisted collectivisation of the reindeer herds (though a few Yakuts were shipped west to camps on the notorious White Sea Canal). Political integration of the Siberians into the Soviet system has been relatively gradual on the whole, moving through phases of clan based and migratory soviets to the present system common throughout the U.S.S.R.

The line between imposed disadvantage and preferred isolation is sometimes a fine one. For the most part, Siberians share in both the rights and vulnerabilities of other Soviet citizens. The most basic right in this context is the right to be recognised as a distinct nationality entitled to a special administrative unit within the Soviet Union, within which aboriginal language and identity have a special status. The greatest vulnerability is common to other Soviet groups; major decisions affecting political, economic and social life are made in Moscow, largely by Russians. The sphere of local and aboriginal authority is very narrow. And the domination of Russians, and secondarily other Slavs, produces a definite "cap" on the mobilization of all minority *cadre*, including Siberians. The concentration of aboriginals in traditional occupations may reflect stereotyping and channeled opportunity as well as local preference. Many traditional cultural and religious practises have been suppressed. On the other hand, such policies as the use of native language for at least some initial schooling and the emphasis on development of histories and literatures for aboriginals, have reinforced aboriginal identity, although they are now being phased out. The pressures for aboriginal assimilation are formidable. They range from stress on the advantages of Russianisation for career advancement and migration away from northern Siberia, to popular propaganda about the superiority of Russian Soviet culture, to suppression of certain aspects of traditional identity (e.g., nomadism, the clan system). These pressures inevitably develop greater cumulative weight over time and with more constant and intensive interaction between Russians and aboriginals. Ultimately a "Soviet" identity is intended to replace all local nationalisms. In the meantime, the design of a minority policy "National in form, Socialist in content" is seen as a vehicle for the erosion of separate identities and statuses. To the extent that Siberians continue to hold on to their traditional languages and identities, this implies a basic tension between them and the Russian state. It is highly unlikely to express itself in violence or even overt protest, but rather in simple persistence.

Besides the general pressures towards assimilation inherent in the modern world, there are probably two main sources of threat to aboriginal identity. The first is pressure from the Russian population, which now outnumbers aboriginals in all their designated administrative units and which is already expressing dissatisfaction with native preference. The second is an acceleration and intensification of the pressures for Russianisation, including a possible decommissioning of the aboriginal administrative units (for which there is precedent) and their merger into the RSFSR. For complex reasons growing out of the special conjunction of history, political philosophy, geography, culture, and demographics in Siberia, aboriginal peoples there are probably in a better position to survive as distinct peoples in the modern world than most aboriginals elsewhere. Both because of and in spite of Soviet policies, the Yakuts and at least some of the "Small Peoples" are likely to survive both the 20th century and the evolution of Soviet nationality policy.

Frances Svensson

BIBLIOGRAPHY

Allworth, Edward (ed), *Soviet Nationality Problems*, Columbia University Press, New York, 1971
Goldhagen, Erich (ed), *Ethnic Minorities in the Soviet Union*, Praeger, New York, 1968
Kolarz, Walter, *The Peoples of the Soviet Far East*, George Philip and Son, London 1954
Levin, M.G. and L.P. Potapov, *The Peoples of Siberia*, University of Chicago Press, Chicago, 1964
MacDonald, R.S.J., *The Arctic Frontier*, University of Toronto Press, Toronto, 1966
Mowat, Farley, *The Siberians*, Penguin, New York and Harmondsworth, 1970
Semyonov, Yuri, *The Conquest of Siberia*, Routledge and Kegan Paul, London, 1944
Svensson, Frances, "The Final Crisis of Tribalism: Comparative Ethnic Policy on the American and Russian Frontiers" in *Ethnic and Racial Studies*, Vol. 1, No. 1, London, 1978
Uvachan, V.N., *The Peoples of the North and Their Road to Socialism* Progress Publishers, Moscow, 1975

2 Aleut and Alaskan Native Society in Transition

Alaska, the 49th and largest state of the American Union, lies to the west of Canada reaching across to the eastern extremities of the Soviet Union. It is not attached to the U.S. physically, but in the past ten years has been swept forcefully into American culture and economy. From 1741 until 1867 it formed part of the expanding Russian empire. In 1867 it was purchased by the U.S and initially named Seward's Folly, after the man who promoted the deal. It became a judicial land district in 1884, and achieved statehood in 1959. The Aleut Islands of Agattu, Atta and Kiska were the site of the only invasion of U.S. territory since the British burned Washington in 1812, when the Japanese captured them in the course of World War II. Thereafter Alaska achieved an unanticipated strategic importance resulting in the development of the Alaskan Highway and several air bases. Today, of its estimated population of 382,000, less than one eighth is thought to be native to Alaska. The vast majority of migrants have moved there since 1950 (there was a 5:1 male/female ratio until 1970, which has not wholly adjusted) and 80,000 or more military personnel.

The true Alaskans may be divided into three groups: the Aleuts, the Eskimos and the Indians. The Alaskan peninsula is thought to be the bridge by which all pre-Columbian inhabitants of the Americas crossed in successive migrations from the Asian continent. The Alaskan Indians belong to the later migrations of 8000 to 15,000 years ago, but the Eskimos and Aleuts came later still, between 3000 and 8000 years ago. The first Russian geographic explorers were quickly followed by their countrymen in search of land, furs, wealth and souls. Their main impact was in the Aleut islands which arch south and east across the Bering Sea — it was Bering who "discovered" them. They are bleak, foggy lands, frostless but prone to high winds or deep fog. There the inhabitants, who call themselves *Unangan* (people), were self-sufficient, their economy based on hunting a variety of seals, whales, sea-lions and sea-otters, as well as shore-line crustacea and birds. They lived in semi-subterranean houses built up and roofed with sods, and buried their dead in the numerous volcanic caves about the islands. In a hundred years, force of arms (the first Russian governor was particularly brutal) and disease reduced the Aleut population from 16,000 to less than 1,500; today there are still less than 4,000. Some 300 live on the Commander Islands which remain attached to the Soviet Union; in the absence of the uncontrolled economic exploitation that has affected Alaska in the past twenty years, they are now thought to be faring comparatively well. Aleut culture was, unlike any other, heavily overlaid by Russian. The villages and towns scattered through the Aleut Islands, and even here and there on the mainland, are marked by domed Orthodox churches, and the Aleuts now have a strong tradition of male voice choral hymn singing. A Cyrillic alphabet was designed in 1830 for the Aleut language.

Eskimo and Aleut languages belong to the same family, but are mutually unintelligible. The Eskimos (*inuit*) may be divided into Inupiak and Yupik speakers in Alaska. The isolation of semi-nomadic Eskimo family bands even led to semi-dialects developing within these bands. There is no tribal structure as such, but Eskimos are named after the regions in which they live and the economy off which they live: South Alaskan (salmon), West Alaskan (seals etc) (North Alaskan (caribou) and Bering Strait (walrus, whales). The physical strength and technical ability, for which they were noted, were essential to their survival. Collective responsibility and loyalty underlay the social and legal order, that was predominantly practical. The Eskimos lived and hunted in the inlets and coasts of Arctic Alaska and some groups lived further inland, hunting and surviving off caribou. They lived in skin tents in the summer, and sod and driftwood houses in the winter. They were overall the least affected of the three native societies by the Russian colonisers, although competition between Russian, American and British fur-trappers was intense and wide-spread during the nineteenth century. Of the 3,000 caribou-hunters only about 50 survive today. The impact on the population since 1867 has been great, with measles, common colds, tuberculosis and syphilis taking its toll of the Eskimos whose unique genetic constitution and metabolism could cope with the severe conditions of Arctic life, but not with white man's diseases. Alaska became a magnet in the 1880s and 1890s for prospectors for gold, copper, and silver. In the last ten years it has become, of course, the largest source of U.S. oil. The Eskimos lost their source of subsistence, and their pride, while true opportunities for stable employment were not opened to compensate.

Indian culture was, before the impact of the white man, tightly hierarchical. The overall language root is now known as *Na Denê*, of which the largest group is Athabascan, to which most subgroups in Alaska belong. The Tlingit who live along the southern coast of Alaska, originally reaching down into California, were "wealthy, artistic and fierce." They had a rigid caste system, which included a slave class, and a monotheistic faith supported by lesser spirits. They put up considerable resistance to the Russians, who sought to administer Alaska from their territory. They lived off both agriculture and fishing. A rather gentler sub-group is the Haida. Further inland, along the Yukon and its tributaries lived the hunting and salmon-fishing Tinneh, who have been assimilated, for good or ill, to a greater extent than the Tlingit. Meanwhile the salmon industry has become a multi-million dollar export business without their participation, except at a low-level.

In the 1880s formal education was extended to Alaska, and with it a considerable increase in missionary activity and translations of the Bible into Inupiak for a basic reading and moral textbook. But even well-intentioned efforts to bring Western customs and education can be derogatory towards indigenous culture. The sudden wrenching of a child from the environment where ancient interpersonal values of non-aggression and non-competitiveness contrast with the white image of educational and business success. When "Mother Goose replaces the indigenous songs, stories, legends and myths", the child will be invalidated, along with his "past, his parents and most of his experiential world". Indeed the Indian language, potlach ceremonies and music were consistently derogated after the establishment of missionary and trader settlements in Alaska. It reached the extent where even the Constitution of the Alaska Native Brotherhood specified that "only English-speaking members of the native residents of the Territory of Alaska are eligible for membership".

Subsequently, a dramatic social reversal in the use of native music and language has come about. With the development of the Native Land Claims Movement, it became politic to be a native culturally as well as genetically. The movement grew in response to the surge of immigrants to Alaska in the wake of oil discoveries in the area. This surge of latter-day frontiersman was racist, exploitive and armed with myths about American greatness that swept aside any thoughts of indigenous greatness and the culture of the continent. When the Alaskan pipeline was proposed, there was a strong outcry from ecological conservationists, but the NLCM was also able to lay claims for recognition, and for compensation. The Bureau of Indian Affairs in Washington, which was responsible for administering Indian, Eskimo and

Aleut welfare, has never been an effective defender of indigenous rights, and, to a large extent, has been overwhelmed by the tremendous upsurge in indigenous protest across the entire U.S. The Native Land Claims Act of 1971 was a unique recognition of native presence, granting 11% of the state (40 million acres) in fee simple and U.S. $462 million in compensation. "For the first time since white contact, the potential now exists for solving the terrible problems of poverty, powerlessness and exclusion assailing most natives of Alaska", said one commentator. It pales beside the $100 million annual income of the salmon packing industry, or the $101 forestry, $8 million furs, or, of course, the oil itself, but it was a constructive gesture by the U.S. government in a strategically sensitive area of immense growth potential.

Some form of economic self-determination is long-overdue, although pessimists like to claim the money is being squandered. In a comparative study of two Aleut villages, the differential degree of control over the sources of livelihood, production and consumption reflected the power and self-interest of the whites. Only where the Aleut were able to wield countervailing power, not necessarily linked to numbers, could they mitigate the devastating effects of racism and economic exploitation. The fishing and whaling industry is hardly in the hands of these indigenous fishermen at all. In recent years, the outcry of conservationists against whaling — aimed primarily at the ubiquitous Japanese whaling fleets — has been resented by the Aleuts. Much of their livelihood used to depend on a limited annual catch, and they protest that this should not be subsumed into an annual U.S. quota, most of which, if not all, would be used up by large mercantile interests. Their protest was international, marking perhaps the first time that the interests of this small group had been noted. The question, however, remains open. The future of Alaska likewise remains open. These abused and diminished people have regained some pride, but the strength of American commerce is such that, despite the gains in kind and money, the native communities in Alaska will have to continue to struggle not to be forgotten as full American citizens with a right to life and to a quality of life of their own choosing.

Tvk

BIBLIOGRAPHY

Collins, H.B., *Arctic Area*, 1954
Hughes, C.C., "Under Four Flags: Recent Culture Change Among the Eskimos" in *Current Anthropology* Vol. 6, No. 3, 1965
Johnston, Thomas F., "Alaskan Native Social Adjustment and the Role of Eskimo and Indian Music", in *Journal of Ethnic Studies*, Vol. 3, No. 4, 1976
Jones, Dorothy M., *Aleuts in Transition: A Comparison of Two Villages*, University of Washington Press, 1976

3   The Amanas and Hutterites in the American West

When one thinks of the American and Canadian West, cowboys, Indians, mounties, hardy lumberjacks and strong-willed farm families and miners immediately come to mind. However there is a different side to the North American West than portrayed by such rugged individualists. During the 19th century several sects of German and Central European pietists and Anabaptists settled in the American west. These groups were and are communal, collective or cooperative in structure. Their strength and endurance lay not in personal achievement but in community solidarity. The most famous of these groups are the Amanas and the Hutterites.

The Amanas or Amanaites take their name from their religious sect, the Community of True Inspiration. Rooted in European mysticism and the Pietist movements of the 16th and 17th centuries, the Amanas came to America too in 1842 to avoid persecution in Germany, Austria, France and Switzerland. 800 members entered the United States and briefly settled in Buffalo, New York before moving on to the Iowa River Valley in east central Iowa. In Iowa, they established seven colonies, each based on their farming communities in the Old World. Each of these communities and their accompanying farmland has in excess of 20,000 acres. By dominating the entire northeast corner of Iowa County, the Amanas have preserved their cultural, social and economic solidarity.

The Amanas lived under a communal system until 1932, when their leaders changed the socio-economic base into one of cooperative capitalism. The result was the formation of a number of Amana companies and the spread of carefully-monitored industry into the area. Around this same time the Amanas modified their life-style and moral system to fit into the mainstream of the rural middle of America. Unlike other "old order" sects such as the Mennonites and Amish in Pennsylvania, the Amanas dress, pay taxes and are publically educated like other Americans. They have accepted the conveniences of modern society. They differ from other Americans in that they speak German as well as English, live in virtually unpenetrated communities and subscribe to the mystical beliefs of their forefathers. Their festivals and cuisine closely resemble that of Germany. The most binding unit of Amana culture is the Amana Society. In 1932 in the middle of the depression, the Amana communities found themselves 400,000 dollars in debt. They reorganised by splitting church and state matters. Economic matters were turned over to the Amana Society. In turn the Amana Society developed co-operative ventures and issued every member one free share of stock in their closed corporation. Valued at $81 in 1932, today each share is worth more than $20,000. The co-operative societies extended beyond the farm to include woollen mills and furniture manufacturing and more recently electrical goods (Amana refrigerators and cookers). This prosperity is the major reason for Amana solidarity. Within their communities, unemployment, crime and labour disputes are unknown. All share the rights, responsbilities and profits and today over 10,000 Amanas enjoy the fruits of their labours with only minimal misunderstanding from their neighbours. To them the "old order" has learned just enough from the new to not only endure but prosper and develop.

Farther west in the Dakotas, Montana and the three plains provinces of Canada live the Hutterites. The Hutterites are members of an Anabaptist sect similar to the Amish of Pennsylvania. Fleeing central Europe and the Ukraine in the 1870's, the Hutterites settled in South Dakota, North Dakota and Montana

where they became large-scale farmers and ranchers. The Hutterite groups are best characterised by large families, communal
organisations with sexual segregation, plain clothing and religious
schooling. Like the Amanas however, the Hutterites have
accepted many modern conveniences, particularly those related
to agriculture, transport and electrification.

Hutterite religion is based on the group's communal order,
stern sexual and age restrictions, strict pacifism and strong group
spirit. Their colonies are sub-divided into three types: *Dariusleut,
Lehrerleut* and *Schmiedeleut*   The Dariusleut is composed of
59 separate colonies in Montana, Alberta and Saskatchewan
(with one in Washington as well). The Lehrerleut has 37 colonies
in Montana, Saskatchewan and Alberta. Finally the Schmiedeleut
has 68 colonies in Manitoba, North Dakota, South Dakota and
Minnesota. Each colony is seldom larger than 100 persons and
the total Hutterite population in both the United States and
Canada is roughly 20,000. Each group speaks a slightly different
dialect of German, originating from Moravia, Slovakia, Tran-
sylvania and the western Ukraine, of the Austro-Hungarian
Empire.

In North America, the Hutterites have not realised the earthly
paradise of the Amanas. In fact discrimination against the sect
is still widespread. During the First World War, American
Hutterites encountered numerous problems. They refused to
participate in the war or in the war effort. Their neighbours,
angered by their refusal to buy war bonds, their resistance of the
draft and their general lack of patriotism, raided their cattle and
sheep herds and burned their buildings. Some draft-age men
were imprisoned. Several died at Fort Leavenworth federal prison
in Kansas. By the end of the First World War, mass migration
of Hutterites to Canada had begun and only after the end of the
Second World War did groups of Hutterites return to the United
States. Memories of the war and exodus to Canada linger and
few Hutterites or Anglos, as their neighbours are called, will
ever forget. This bitterness is re-inforced by lack of communication between Hutterite colonies and the outside world. Few
Anglos are interested in this and due to a ban on radios and
televisions the Hutterites know surprisingly little about life in
the outside world.

Neither the Amanas or the Hutterites have membership in
Europe anymore and together they may be called the "old order

Germans" of the North American West. In many ways they are similar to one another and to the Pennsylvania Deutsch groups. However both groups have been hampered with well-meaning comparisons. Neither group has significant political power on any level higher than the township, but the Amanas and the Hutterites have influenced American and Canadian social and moral thinking greatly. In spite of their size, the Amanas and Hutterites have contributed much to pacifist, progressive, social-ist, co-operative and communal movements in North America. Their perseverance has brought them both rewards and tribu-lations. Due to high birthrates among both groups, Amana and Hutterite power can be expected to rise on local levels in Iowa, eastern South Dakota, South central Manitoba and southern Alberta. What effect this potential may have is largely dependent on how much political activity is fostered and how great an impact modern society will have on the "old order" in the next two decades.

Randall Fegley

BIBLIOGRAPHY

Ahlstrom, Sydney, *A Religious History of the American People*, Yale University Press, New Haven, 1972

Allard, William A., "The Hutterites, Plain People of the West", *National Geographic*, July 1970

Babb, Laura L., "Iowa's Enduring Amana Colonies", *National Geographic*, December 1975

Holloway, Mark, *Heavens on Earth: Utopian Communities in America*, Dover Press, New York, 1966

Salisbury, W. Steward, *Religion in American Culture*, Home-wood Ill, 1964

Wilson, Bryan, *Religious Sects*, London, 1970

4 Background to the Ethnic Problems in Mauritania

Recent fighting over the fate of the Western Sahara and subsequent instability in the West African Islamic Republic of Mauritania have brought to the fore ethnic tensions which threaten the unity of the nation created only twenty years ago. The issue is often presented in terms of "white" northerners of Arabo-Berber descent versus "black" southerners, but in reality the issue is far more complex and can be understood only in a historical context.

Before the French colonised this vast, largely arid area of the Sahara, the sparse population was organised in distinctive tribes. In the more fertile Senegal River Basin the tribes were an integral part of those in present day Senegal, Mali, and Niger: Wolof, Fulani, Toucouleur, Malinki. Descended from the peoples of the great black empires of the region, they had their own unwritten languages and customs and had more or less dark skins and negroid features. Mainly farmers but also herdsmen, they lived in villages and tended to have permanent homes. North of the river area were two main groups of tribes, both essentially nomadic and interdependent. The first, known as the "Warriors" were mainly light-skinned, Arab-featured descendants of the Ben Hassan tribes who invaded across from the Yemen in the 13th century; they built up a highly-structured relationship with the "Monastic" or "Scholar" tribes, Islamised Berber in origin and native to the region. Slightly darker-skinned, these tribes paid tribute to certain Warrior tribes, providing intellectual and spiritual support in return for physical and political protection. Some intermarriage took place and a dialect of Arabic, *Hassaniyah*, became the common language, so that both groups were finally known as the "Moors" or "Whites".

Over the centuries all Moors took "black" slaves from the

south and east and used them for manual work. These slaves eventually spoke only Hassaniyah and took on the customs of the Moors. Some were freed and became *Haratin*, even in some cases establishing their own, separate tribes not easily distinguised in structure and custom from the Moorish tribes and quite distinct from the southern, black tribes. These northern tribal groupings fought, made alliances and traded with the black tribes in the Senegal River Valley area. Islam was sometimes a unifying factor, and inevitably, intermarriage and concubinage eventually led to a situation in which actual skin colour meant little; tribal membership and language were far more significant.

The French colonised the whole area in the early twentieth century but for many years barely penetrated the difficult lands north of the River Senegal Basin. Calling the colony French West Africa, they established the capital, St. Louis, at the delta of the River Senegal and had far more contact with the sedentary Wolof, Toucouleur, Fular and Malinki peoples along the river. The fact that these peoples' languages were purely oral meant that it was relatively easy to establish French as the administrative language, and schools for teaching it could be set up in the towns and villages. The nomadic tribes to the north were far harder to reach and they remained largely hostile. They had classical Arabic as a written language and long traditions of literature and education. Even when eventually "pacified" many continued stubbornly to resist French civilisation; some tribal chiefs went so far as to substitute slave boys for the sons they were supposed to send to the "School for Chiefs' Sons" on the River.

For these reasons, when the Republic of Mauritania was created in the late 1950s with the River Senegal as its southern border, and given independence in 1960, it was in many ways easier for the black southern populations to cope with administrative work, all of which was carried out in French. Their sedentary habits and their readiness (in contrast to many Moors) to carry out manual tasks gave them some advantages in the circumstances.

At this time the Moors were estimated at 75 of the population of one and a half million; this included *Hassaniyah*-speaking black slaves, automatically freed under the Constitution created at Independence. Many Moors resented formal integration with the "black" South — although the fertility of the River Senegal Basin was all important to some of them during dry seasons in the north. A tendency towards integration with Morocco was rejected, but a number of Moors felt strongly that their traditions and culture were being threatened by the use of the French language for education and administration.

Deeply religious and also perhaps looking towards the best possible terms with the oil-rich Arab nations to the east, there was growing Moorish insistence that Arabic should be the national language instead of French. This was seen as a threat to their prosperity by the peoples of the River Senegal Valley, many of whom now worked and traded in the centre and north of the country. Although also deeply committed to Islam, their religious education had not been so rigorous as the Moors' and their command of classical Arabic was sketchy. They felt too that the Moors still regarded them as potential slaves, good only for manual work, and that they were being repressed politically. The first President, Ould Daddah (a Moor from a "Monastic" tribe) went to considerable lengths to propagate a policy of non-racism and proportionate representation in every public sphere, but common attitudes and behaviour did not always reflect this policy.

When Arabic teaching was first introduced into schools and colleges, non-*Hassaniyah*-speaking black students objected strongly, feeling disadvantaged, and in 1966 violent fighting broke out in many towns and villages. Somehow the troubles subsided and bilingual (Arabic-French) education was established in schools — at vast cost, for two teachers had to be engaged for each class. Arabic was now technically the national language, but as French was still used almost exclusively for administrative and government work, few real problems emerged. The financial advantages of membership of the Arab League were obvious to all.

In fact, during the relatively prosperous years of the mid-70s, the ethnic problem was not prominent and Ould Daddah continued to make efforts to minimise ethnic and tribal considerations in public life.

Problems began to emerge once more in 1975, when Mauritania made an alliance with Morocco, with whom she signed an agreement to partition the territory lying between them, then hastily being de-colonised by Spain. Many people from the south of Mauritania felt that alliance with Morocco increased the danger of "Arabo-Berber" domination and, when fighting broke out and Mauritania was forced to engage heavy expenses for warfare, they questioned the wisdom of ruining the country's economy for the sake of yet more desert land. Moreover, many of the soldiers being wounded and killed by the Algerian-backed Polisario Front were black southerners, who had been led to volunteer by their need for at least a subsistence wage following the disastrous droughts in the River Senegal area, and unemployment resulting from the war-crippled economy.

Nevertheless, some politicians, army officers and businessmen from the south were not against the war and it was not until the military Coup d'Etat of July 1978 that the ethnic issue took on serious proportions. Rumours spread that the new government, under the leadership of Lt. Col. Moustapha Ould Salek, was in favour of ethnic discrimination and even slavery and, although these rumours were strongly denied, there is little doubt that the new leadership's commitment to the elimination of racism and tribalism lacked the fervour of Ould Daddah's.

At about the same time, some southerners began to challenge the results of the national population census conducted in 1977 and 1978. They alleged that the suppressed returns showed that the 75-25 "white-black" split was a myth — and the populations were now equal. This increased their resentment and led to the forming of ethnic pressure groups and demands for the rehabilitation of their languages, as in Senegal. Meanwhile, alarmed at the sight of 9,000 Moroccan troops only miles away to the north, President Senghor of Senegal at one point went so far as to allude to possible 'self-determination' for the peoples of the northern River Senegal bank, all of whom have the closest possible family ties with the Senegalese.

Clashes, recalling 1966, occurred early in 1979, and finally the 17 members of the 81-strong national Consultative Committee resigned in protest at inadequate representation. It was against this uneasy background that Lt. Col. Ahmed Ould Bouceif quietly took effective power on 6 April 1979, although retaining Ould Salek as nominal president.

The new leadership withdrew later in the year, from the Sahara conflict, abandoning their claims and the desert to the Moroccans. If Mauritania succeeds in returning to a more peaceful existence, it will need to build up economic prosperity, and also cope with the problems of a diversified population in

which a delicate balance must be maintained for violent conflict
to be avoided.

J. Lunnon

BIBLIOGRAPHY

Diego, Charles, *Sahara*, 1935
Gerteiny, Alfred G., *Mauritania*, 1967
Marty, Paul, *Etude sur l'Islam maure*, 1966

5   China's Forty Millions

At the inauguration of Communist rule in the Peoples Republic
of China, the significance of the national minorities was not
underestimated. A principal objective of the Chinese Communist
Party was to eliminate foreign influence from China's frontier
regions to the North, West and South, where the greatest minority
concentrations could be found. At the same time, as the 1953
Census revealed, 6% of the population — the national minorities
— occupied 60% of the land area, much of it wild remote and
barren, but with coal and oil in Sinkiang, tin in Yunnan, copper
in Szechwan. Today, there are about 40 million people of national
minority descent belonging to 55 different groups, whose 40-odd
languages stem from 3 different linguistic families; 10 million
are Moslem, the remaining 94% are Han Chinese.

A *General Programme for the People's Republic of China for
the Implementation of National Regional Autonomy* was issued
in 1952, promising self-government, use of language in private
and public life, "internal reform", use of income from the
exploitation of local resources and incorporation in local militia.
These are all particular areas of dispute in minority-majority
relations in any multiethnic or multinational state. Cadres or
administrators from the minority areas were trained in Peking
from the early fifties, to ensure rapid "social transformation" in

these strategically sensitive areas. While industrial units remain concentrated in the East as does the dense urban proletariat; regional economic development has been particularly important in minority areas (55% of the First Five Year Plan), both to win the hearts and minds of the potentially dissident groups, and to feed China's vast population as a whole.

The main concentrations of national minorities have been reflected in the establishment of five Autonomous Regions. *Kwangsi-Chuang* lies on the border with Vietnam in the South, where there are 6.6 million *Chuang*, the largest group overall. *Sinkiang-Uighur*, a mountainous area in the West, on the Soviet border, is the largest, where there are 3.7 million *Uighur*, and a particularly significant minority of *Kazakhs*. *Ningsia-Hui*, where there are 3.6 million Moslem *Hui*, is the smallest of all China's regions or provinces whose existence, nestling close to Inner Mongolia, perhaps reflects *Hui* support for Mao Tse Tung during the Civil War. Buddhist *Tibet* (2.8 million) was absorbed in 1959, while Inner Mongolia in the North (1.3 million Mongols) was the earliest established in 1947. These figures are from official sources published in 1977, but may be considered conservative; another sanctioned source gives figures that sometimes double these. It is not possible here to give a detailed account of numbers, anthropological origins, nor the historic internal migrations of each group, partly because there is a great dearth of information on "China's Forty Millions" in the West, and partly because they are still subject to academic argument, while most visitors to China, even in recent years, have been restricted to the Eastern provinces; only lastly for reasons of space. The borders of the Autonomous Regions do not necessarily encompass all the nationals of these largest groups, nor are they exclusive to them. Internally they may be divided into autonomous *chous* (districts) — Sinkiang, for example has 24 — *tsien* (counties), and smaller administrative units, reflecting the ethnic population patterns.

In the large *South Western provinces* between Sinkiang, Tibet and Kwangsi-Chuang — land-locked *Tsinghai* and *Szechwan*; *Yunnan* on the border with Burma, Laos and Vietnam; *Kweichow* — there are considerable concentrations of the smaller groups, as well as 2.5 million *Miao* (Meo or Hmong), 1.25 million *Pui*, and over half a million each of *Tung*, *Yao* and *Tai*. In *Yunnan* 26 groups are represented. Traditionally regarded as primitive

by successive Han autocracies, many moved south to avoid
repression. Some groups were enslaved, with a caste system
evolving among the *Yi*. Many of these groups are also to be found
outside China in "the Golden Triangle" of Burma, Thailand
West of the Mekong, Laos and Vietnam.

The third area of national minority concentration is in the
North East, formerly *Manchuria* (earlier seat of imperial power),
a pocket between Mongolia, the Soviet Union and Korea, now
divided into the provinces of *Kirin, Heilungkiang* and *Liaoning*.
The *Yen-Pien* autonomous district accommodates 1.1 million,
but minorities today represent only 6% of the local population.
The North East has the bulk of provincial industrial development
finance under China's first 5 year plans, and Han migration to
the region has been considerable.

The inherent dilemmas in China's minority policies were most
obvious in *Sinkiang*, where the Kazakh stock herders had strong
social ties with the Soviet Union, and whose trade and communications were almost exclusively with Soviet Central Asia.
Although Soviet technical help in the 1950s was important to
China as a whole, and the Sinkiang oil-fields in particular, there
was a strong desire to restrict Soviet influence in the area — in
direct conflict with the proletariat internationalism of the Chinese
Community Party, and the anti-imperialism of its message. Most
of Sinkiang had never been subject to any traditional Chinese
dynasty, and its valleys were a sanctuary for Uighur farm settlers
during the Chi'ing period, while the wilder stock-herding Kazakh
and Kirghiz clans roamed and competed and traded at will,
evading Russian imperialism from the West. Nor did the Kuom-
intang (Nationalist Government) ever fully extend its influence
into the area.

Probably containing the most distinct people — historically,
culturally and psychologically — from the remainder of China
this Moslem region was subject to an intense "Sinification"
during the 1950s, both to offset Soviet influence (particularly
among the Kazakhs) and to speed the reorganisation of clans
into productive units, amenable to administrative and social
control. The Kazakhs were subjected to the most intensive reo-
rientation of all national minorities. "It was difficult to persuade
non-Chinese minorities that it was in their interest to struggle
for a prosperous China", writes one observer, who views the
autonomy programme within China as a "formal structure to

capture the imagination of the inhabitants, while the party actually made decisions". The cultivated area of Sinkiang was doubled and eventually, as in Inner Mongolia, all nomads and herders settled and "modernised". Han immigration in all areas has been intensive — partly to relieve population stress in the East. (Han population in Sinkiang grew from 6.2% in 1953 to 31.2% by 1970; in Tsinghai from 50.7% to 66.5% and elsewhere by figures of 3-4%.) Immigration, it must be added, is usually by males leaving their families if they have them, and not always voluntary. Chinese publications admit to Han chauvinism, but minority nationalist sentiment roused, even among the Uighur, can always be ascribed to anti-CCP "bourgeios or reactionary" tendencies, and its leadership treated accordingly: the repression of Kazakh leadership has been reported particularly strong. By 1960 Sino-Soviet relations reached a crisis and the Soviet technicians left China. In 1962, in a less well-known, incident 50,000 Kazakhs (and probably 16,000 resident Russians) left China for the Kazakh SSR, and the border was closed, sealing Sinkiang to China. (Even at this stage the U.S. Secretary of State thought it possible that Sinkiang might be detached from China by the U.S.S.R.).

During the political upheavals at the end of the sixties and more recently, the minorities policies have not appeared to change. The "Hundred Flowers" movement probably made little impact, and while the Cultural Revolution may have unleashed Han prejudices in some areas, some groups in the remote South West may have been oblivious to it. The Cultural Revolution was intended to eradicate the "four olds": religious beliefs, traditional culture, customs and habits, which were entrenched among the minorities. Language usage has never been in dispute and for as long as politic, minorities using non-Chinese script (Cyrillic, Arabic, Mongol, Thai) have been permitted to continue. The codification of un-written minority languages into Chinese script has been achieved for most, alongside the simplification of Mandarin to make it nationally intelligible. Teaching has been in both languages (although Han commentators point out that mother-tongue learning sets children back two school years) but education in the majority language is universally the key to advancement. The government claims a 90% literacy rate where there would have been 90% illiteracy 30 years ago. Malaria has been eliminated in some areas, and bare foot doctors extended to minority regions. Today, it is claimed that 80% of cadres in minority areas are from the minorities, of whom 16% are women. If this were the case it would both reduce areas of tension between Han and "the barbarians", and decrease Peking's formal control of the autonomous areas which has been through Han party officials, technicians, doctors etc.

Some social reforms may only now be reaching the *South West*: for example family planning was not enforced during the 1950s, while marriage and land reforms (which were vital in the northern areas where footbinding, female subjugation and land-lessness had been particularly strong) have been delayed. Women among the Pai (a Tibeto-Burman group) for instance had higher status already than Han women, while some groups had been slave-subjects to the War Lords and there remains strong resent-ments against Han "interference" after centuries of forced con-cubinage or "marriage". This in part explains the limited effect so far on local culture in the south west, where marriage customs are elaborate and intrinsic to minority societies. Villages remain insular, scattered and ethnically interspersed, practising cut-and-burn agriculture, growing buck wheat and dry rice. Areas that have converted to wet rice have been those where land reform has been achieved (or the land ownership already traditionally in local hands rather than subject to tenancies) and this is deemed a sign of greater national assimilation. Many Chuang, in par-ticular, whose economic base has always been sounder than other ethnic minorities, identify themselves, and are identified as belonging to the majority. Mineral resources in Kwangsi are relatively rich and accessible and alongside its agricultural output, it has not been regarded as a "problem" province, although the recent conflict with Vietnam may have affected its peaceful status. Mining areas are generally reported to be managed by the autonomous area or local commune.

Inner Mongolia, in which the Han were already a sizeable minority, has been subject to large-scale migration, but *Heilun-kiang* next to the Soviet border in the North East even more so. (It also received the lion's share of the first Five Year Plan). The nomadic groups remaining among the Mongols have been "suc-cessfully" settled, not without conflict, and land reform was completed quickly. Mongols have a strong system of communal ownership and public service; many are still Buddhists. The term Hui is deemed to mean Moslem Han, rather than a separate ethnic grouping, much as Manchu is a political term for the descendants of those who used to hold power: neither fact is beyond dispute, but it allows for less overt discrimination towards them from among the Han. In the North East the groupings are small (Nanai, Ulchi, Udegoy, Orochi, Oroki) and family based. The 1975 Constitution for the Peoples' Republic re-iterated in Article 38 that the "organs of self-government of autonomous regions, autonomous chous, and autonomous tsien are peoples' congresses and revolutionary committees". Article 40 emphasised the role of the cadres to "actively support and assist all the national minorities in their social revolution and construction and thus advance their social, economic and cultural development". Article 46 guarantees the freedom to believe and practise religion, and not to believe, as well as to propagate atheism.

The somewhat schizophrenic attitude of the Chinese government to the national minorities is likely to continue. Mistakes are admitted, especially in the attitude of some over-zealous Han cadres, but there is unlikely to be any sudden change of direction. No political system has yet solved the problem of its institutional — and personal — relationships with minorities.

TvK

BIBLIOGRAPHY

Dreyer Teufel, June, *China's Forty Millions*, Harvard, Cambridge, 1976

FitzGerold, C.P., *The Southern Expansion of the Chinese People*, London, 1972

"Scripts for Minorities", *Far Eastern Economic Review*, Hong Kong 1962

"National Minorities: The Policy", *China News Analysis*, Hong Kong, 1965

Orleans, Leo O., *Every Fifth Child: the Population of China*, Eyre Methuen, London, 1972

Mosely, George, *A Sino-Soviet Cultural Frontier*, Harvard East Asian Monographs, 1966

Wang, Shu-tang, *China: Land of Many Nationalities*, Peking, 1955

Wilson, Dick, *A Quarter of Mankind*, London, 1966

6 The Constant Conflict in Chad

Locked between the deserts of Libya, Niger, Nigeria, Sudan, the Central African Republic and the more verdant border of Cameroun, Chad is one of the largest and poorest countries in Africa. The conflict that has spluttered continuously for 13 years, locking 31% of the national budget into military expenditure, has so many elements that peace is almost unimaginable. This area was the last to be colonised by the French at the turn of the century and the impact was indubitably devastating. Within the first 25 years of French rule, the population is estimated to have dropped by up to 63% in some areas. It has never recovered: today's 4 million remains less than before the French presence. A scandal in its day, the causes included firstly the forced labour recruitment for the railway system being developed in Gabon — one African death per cross-tie, one European death per kilometre was the estimate. Imported disease, particularly small-pox in 1905, Spanish 'flu in 1918, and venereal disease arguably introduced from Europe in the 1920s, took an immense toll. With the introduction of paid "wages", came immediate taxation: male *transfugiés* fled its punitive effects into Sudan, Ethiopia and British Cameroun. The demography was further unbalanced by the use of Chadian forces, predominantly from the Sara tribe, in North Africa, Indo-China and Europe in World War I: most losses were in the apalling transit conditions rather than in the fighting. Famine stalked the women, working the land to keep alive the abandoned villages of children and the old. In the last census in 1965 the balance had just reached 47% men to 53% women.

The fertile tenth of Chad's 495,750 square miles, lies south of the river Chari and here the cultural impact of the French was greatest. Missionary activity converted the nearest tribes to Christianity. In 1964 29% were registered as Christians in 4

Roman Catholic dioceses. The remainder are 41% Muslim, and 30% animist. French remains the official language — there are two others, rooted in the different groupings, as well as Arabic, spoken predominantly in the North and East. In the river basins live the 1 million Sara and their Sudanese (an anthropological not political term) neighbours, such as the Banguirm. Round the northern shores of Lake Chad particularly close to the Niger border, the sedentary Islamic groups (Biltine, Kanem), co-exist with the Saharan nomadic groups (Kanembu); while the Arab Hassaoun and Djoheiha are in the North East; the Tubu (Teda or Ennedi) in the Tibesti massif. The complex legacies of pre-colonial West African empires must be understood, and the strong remaining feudal relationships, closely attached to north-south trading patterns, to be found in the semi-arid savannah and mountainous deserts.

Chad is also on the path of Hajj pilgrims to Mecca from Nigeria and points west, which affects the population structure at any given time, as well as non-monetary or informal trade. The economy is heavily dependent on imports of oil and manu-factured implements (as well as military hardware). France is still Chad's largest trading partner, with Nigeria second. The main export, grown in the more prosperous South, is cotton (72%) with cotton seed oil; while ground nuts are grown for oil: but both are cash crops subject to unreliable world prices. Beef, herded in the central savannah regions, reaches 17% of exports: there are over 4.5 million head of cattle. Ndjadema, the capital (formerly Fort Lamy) is to the east of Lake Chad (a source of fish), astride the only major road — leading eastwards to the Sudan — and between the two predominant cultural systems of Chad. The conflict in Chad, in its simplest form, has been between North and South, Muslim and Christian (or animist), Arab and black African, tradition and modernity, nomad and sedentary agriculturist. It was only in 1965, after the withdrawal of French military administration that the Bokor, Ennedi, and Tibesti regions, with a sparse population of 50,000 came under civilian rule from Fort Lamy as newly formed prefectures. A year later, guerilla forces, particularly among the Tubu, began their opposition to central government. The Chadian army, still composed largely of Sara, was supported from the start by French troops — the Foreign Legion until recently, now replaced by the "paras". Opposition to the tight clench of French interests and

"interference", may be added to the motivation of the Northerners: and in recent years this has attracted Libyan support. The
intricacies of Libyan assistance are interpreted by some observers
both as a proxy war against France and the extension of radical
Muslim hegemony southwards to threaten the flank of the Sudan,
now friendly towards Egypt, Libya's neighbour. In dispute has
been the uranium bearing Ouzon strip on the borders between
Libya and Chad. Other external interests, both selfish and peace-
making, have been expressed by Chad's neighbours, who have
initiated several conferences and truces (Sudan, Nigeria and
lately Congo-Brazzaville) and have attempted to supply peace-
keeping forces to replace the French. Oil has been explored, by
the U.S. Conoco firm, with IMF support. Although quantities
are comparatively slight and production has not yet started, this
will attract further international competition for Chad, who may
benefit little from the discovery. Such economic development as
has occurred so far, has been in the south, where the only hospital
and other services are to be found.

   The President for the first 10 years of Chad's independence
was Toumboulaye, who was removed in 1975 by a military coup
d'etat led by Felix Malhoum. Since that time, the conflict grew,
both as Malhoum's Southern power-base receded — partly cause
and partly effect of much-increased French military involvement
on his side — and the rebellion spread beyond the Tibesti, until
the rebels straddled the Sudan road, when Ati was captured in
1978, thereby threatening Ndjamena. That year, the FROLI-
NAT (Front pour la Liberation Nationale du Tchad) leadership
split, and in an effort at conciliation, the French persuaded
Malhoum to accept Hissene Habre (Frolinat's former leader) as
Prime Minister.

   1979, however, saw the fiercest and cruellest fighting: between
Malhoum's supporters and Habre's, devastating the capital Ndjamena, and allowing Oueddi Goukouni, Frolinat's new leader, to
invade the city. The French announced their withdrawal, and
airlifted civilians out, but remained as a military presence.
Malhoum went into exile, and Habre became President with
Goukoumi as Prime Minister: the "North taking its turn".
Although a government of national unity was declared in November, observers remain sceptical of peace. Ndjamena is a city
deserted of civilians, but occupied by military factions, old enemies
now to be united in a single army, not dominated by the Sara.

The integration of opposing forces is, as in Zimbabwe-Rhodesia, important to the future of the country, but it is also desirable that the troops should be withdrawn from the capital and the tendency to settle old scores eliminated. Withdrawal will be, however, to regional bases and consequently regional loyalties. Elections have been promised in 18 months, but observers predict tension within the labyrinthine factions that form the 11-party government. Each Party, or groupings among them, may also turn back to the regional bases whence they came, or look to Libya or France, for arms and ideological fuel. Yet the resolution of such a conflict requires a conciliatory effort such as this, and the withdrawal of all but the most neutral of interests.

G.A.

BIBLIOGRAPHY

Azevedo, Mario Joaquin, *Sara Demographic Instability as a Consequence of French Colonial Policy in Chad 1890–1940*, University Microfilm, Ann Arbor, 1976
Rodney, Walter, *How Europe Underdeveloped Africa*, Dar-es-Salaam, 1972
Vincent, Jeanne-Francoise, *Le Pouvoir et le Sacre chez les Hadjeray du Tchad*, Editions Anthropos, Paris, 1975
West, Richard, *Brazza of the Congo; European Exploration and Exploitation of French Equatorial Africa*, London, 1972

7 Czechoslovakia: Nationalities and "Normalisation"

Following the defeat of Austria-Hungary in World War I, Czechoslovakia was created an independent unitary republic incorporating Czechs, Slovaks, Magyars (Hungarians), Germans, Poles, Ukrainians and Jews. The Czech and Slovak languages are similar but not identical, and while both peoples are Slav and formed the majority, the establishment of the state was not without resistance from the Slovaks who had aspirations of autonomy. Under the Austro-Hungarian monarchy the Czech provinces, Bohemia and Moravia in the west were contiguous to Germany, with coal and the main East European arms industry, as well as 80–90% of the textile industries. A Czech and German middle-class and industrial proletariat had developed, replacing the feudal supremacy of the Germans, though not removing tension between them.

The Slovaks in the east, on the other hand, inhabited the more rugged terrain and had been culturally and economically stifled by Hungarian landowners. Slovak nationalism developed in the first place as resistance to the Hungarians, and later as a strongly clerical (Roman Catholic) peasant movement, suspicious of the secular centralised character of the new Czechoslovak state.

The first republic recognised no group rights, but individual democratic rights were guaranteed; despite its inauspicious start, these are deemed to have been fairly observed. Land and monetary reform led to greater stability than in Czechoslovakia's neighbours, and the first great leader was a Slovak, Thomas Masaryk. The inter-war years were marked largely by coalition government aiming to include the dissident nationalists in the German Sudetenland and Slovakia. In 1927 a provincial assembly was set up in Slovakia, but it had fewer autonomous powers than those promised a decade before by Masaryk himself in the Pittsburgh agreement.

The population figures below illustrate the great changes in Czechoslovakia's ethnic make-up that were to come:

Nationality	1930	1947	1973
Czechs			9,434,000
	9,689,000	11,090,000	
Slovaks			4,365,000
Germans	3,232,000	250,000	78,000
Hungarians	692,000	600,000	580,000
Russians ⎫ Ruthenians ⎬ Ukrainians ⎭	549,000	100,000	50,000
Poles	82,000	110,000	69,000
Jews	187,000 ⎫	50,000	—
Other	16,000 ⎭		49,000
Gypsies	32,000	(no est)	(220,000 of Slovaks)

Special events at the close of World War II contributed in particular to these dramatic changes: the expulsion of the Germans, the mutual exchange of inhabitants with Hungary, and the surrender of the Carpathian Ukraine to the Soviet Union in 1945. To the hostility between the Czechs and the Germans had been added the threat of secession by the Sudeten areas and the increasing strength of the fascist Sudeten German Party. When Hitler used the Sudeten Germans as an excuse to invade Czechoslovakia, Czech bitterness led to violent reprisals after the war and Allied agreement at Potsdam to the forcible expulsion of the Germans: 1.3 million to the US zone, and 0.78 million to the Soviet zone. Those that remained hoped for patriation to West Germany, and stayed stateless until 1953 when they were unilaterally declared Czechoslovak citizens. Slovaks and repatriates from Hungary, as well as Hungarians themselves, were moved to the Sudeten areas to diffuse the remaining German concentration and to render old threats neutral once and for all.

Germany's invasion in 1938 had caused the collapse of the internal political institutions and democratic structures, and while forcing a form of autonomy on Slovakia (to undermine Czech authority) under German hegemony, paved the way for the Communist takeover in 1948. The Hungarian minority, many of whom sympathised with both "Greater Hungary" aspirations and with the fascist Horthy wartime regime, were also regarded as inimical to the State, and in 1946 a Treaty arranged for the not wholly successful exchange of populations. A quarter of a million Jews had been eliminated after the German invasion, and most of the remainder emigrated to Israel when it was founded. Although no longer a separate nationality group according to the constitution, the number of Gypsies increased dramatically after the war through immense immigration, and there are now an estimated 220,000, most of whom live in Slovakia.

The Czechoslovak citizen since 1948 has been expected to act completely in the spirit of proletarian nationalism. National minorities were deemed to exist no longer; except as a homeland for the Czechs and Slovaks, the constitutional documents made no reference to them. Assimilation was taken for granted, and ties even with neighbouring communist states — Hungary and Poland — discouraged. The 1950s proved to be particularly hard years for the Slovaks, whose national and cultural institutions were disbanded and leaders imprisoned. The 1960 Constitution allowed more flexibility in education and language use, but abolished the Slovak National Council, the Bratislava cabinet and the status of Bratislava as the Slovak capital. The government of Antonin Novotny proved to be the most repressive regime the Slovaks had endured this century. Novotny himself was openly abusive of Slovak leadership and culture, and the purges of the 1950s and early 1960s caused a great deal of resentment between the Czechs and Slovaks. The Hungarians were less affected, and had greater cultural and political freedom — perhaps to add to the harassment of the Slovaks. The Ukrainians and Poles suffered with the others from the administrative rezoning of 1960 and 1961, and their region remained undeveloped industrially, but their cultural associations were not extinguished.

With the accession to power of Alexander Dubcek in January 1968, important changes were made to improve the situation of national minorities. The April Action Plan recognised the necessity of nationality representation in "political and economic and public life in the elected and executive bodies". The Hungarian cultural organisation, *Csemadok*, immediately proposed wide ranging political and administrative changes including a Secretariat of National Minorities. The Ukrainians (despite antagonism between the Greek Catholic and Orthodox groups within) and Polish minorities added their voice to the Hungarian demands. *Matica Slovenksa*, the Slovak cultural association, was revived and actively entered the nationalist struggle — demanding rights for the Slovaks at least equal to those of the Hungarians. Antagonism between the Hungarians and Slovaks was revived, and more Slovaks migrated from Hungarian areas, but there were also a few clashes with Ukrainians over schools. The Germans were less quick to act, but the Gypsies — in turn with less success — made rapid demands of the new politic: they too had suffered intensely under Novotny.

The intervention of the Warsaw Pact countries in August 1968 — opposed in sudden unity by all nationalities, including Czech — forestalled the introduction of these potentially democratic institutions. The new Constitution, hastily drafted and approved in October did, however, define the status of minorities. It was an improvement on past legislation, but the national minorities were dissatisfied. Gustav Husak, who replaced Dubcek, had been an important Slovak leader, imprisoned earlier for "bourgeois nationalism". Under Husak, Slovak culture has flourished but federalism remains a dream. 300,000 members of the communist party, mostly Czechs, have been expelled and the Slovak balance restored to the government. Although few people have been tried for "anti-State activities", the cultural associations have been purged and have lost their independence to the Ministry of Culture. "Normalisation" has suppressed free discussion, very particularly that on the problems of nationalities. The Party remains the political administrative structure meeting Soviet fears and defence needs. The first may well be based on fears of political disintegration rather than liberalisation itself; the latter based on the fact that Czechoslovakia has a wider frontier with West Germany than with the Soviet Union. In May 1971 the Party Congress declared: "The Party will increasingly promote socialist relations between our peoples and the national minorities, as well as the universal Czechoslovakian consciousness in the spirit of both proletarian internationalism and socialist patriotism, mutual respect, co-operation, equality and fraternity. It will fight determinedly to extinguish all expressions of nationalism and chauvinism".

Whether this policy will meet the needs of the nationalities is doubtful. The brief period of democratic hopes opened by Dubcek is remembered particularly by the nationalities as a more realistic attempt.

GA/RF

BIBLIOGRAPHY

Bertsch, Gary K., *Value Change and Political Community: The Multinational Czechoslovak, Soviet and Yugoslav Cases*, London, 1974

King Robert R., *Minorities under Communism*, Cambridge Mass, 1973

Renner H. "The National Minorities on Czechoslovakia After the Second World War" in *Plural Societies* Vol 7 No 1, Spring 1976

Sinanian, Sylva et al, *Eastern Europe in the 1970s*, London 1972

Staar, Richard F., *The Communist Regimes in Eastern Europe*, Stanford, Calif, 1971
Steiner, Eugen, *The Slovak Dilemma*, Cambridge, 1973

8 The Danish Minority in West Germany and the German Minority in Denmark

It is a well established opinion that the hundred year old minority conflict in Schleswig has been settled in such a way that this German–Danish border region may be characterised as a model for the settlement of minority conflicts or at least an example for solving problems of this kind elsewhere in Europe. This is explictly the standpoint of the Schleswig-Holstein Land government, while the previous Prime Minister of Schleswig-Holstein, Herr Kai-Uwe von Hassel, often emphasises the exemplary significance of the Bonn-Copenhagen minority declarations upon which governments in Bonn, Copenhagen and Kiel (the capital of Schleswig-Holstein) agreed in March 1955.

Schleswig is characterised by a mixed German-Danish population and culture that cannot be separated by an exact line. Although the duchy of Schleswig belonged to Denmark until 1864, this was not at issue until the beginning of the 19th century, when the process of modern nation-building started. The effect was that Denmark — under internal nationalist pressures — tried to incorporate Schleswig against strong German opposition, thus abandoning Schleswig's historical connection with the duchy of Holstein, itself related both to Denmark and the German Confederation. The Germans wished to keep Schleswig and Holstein connected and to incoporate both into Germany, while others wanted to gain independence from both sides. This incompatibility of interests admitted no other solution than a division of Schleswig according to the distribution of the two nationalities.

But nationalism (which is in effect nothing other than an integration ideology based on specific values) dominated on both sides, and the impossibility emerged of drawing a clear and undisputed line between both national groups without creating minorities. Instead, a military 'solution' was reached: Prussia incorporated both Schleswig and Holstein. Not until the end of World War I did a referendum in North and Central Schleswig take place (1920) with the result that North Schleswig was ceded to Denmark (by 75,133 to 25,329 votes) and Central Schleswig remained with Germany (by 51,303 to 12,859 votes). Inevitably, two minorities of different size remained on both sides of the border.

Both the Germans in North Schleswig and the Danes in Germany are minorities by will, that is the subjective criterion is decisive as opposed to objective criteria such as language, race or religion. Belonging has been an article of faith. Considering the close relationships between both culture and language a shift in nationality is possible but constitutes a delicate process of socialisation. Scientifically it is necessary but difficult to examine the motivation of members of these groups to find the characteristics of identification with a social group called a 'minority'. Steps into this direction have been taken by Svalastoga/Wolf (1963), Sievers et al (1975), Elklit et al (1978) and J. Zeh (forthcoming). Both minorities may only barely be called ethnic groups ('Volksgruppe').

It is estimated that in the 1970s there are about 15–20,000 Germans in Denmark and about 60–70,000 Danes in Germany including some of the North Frisians who feel close to the Danish minority. (See World Minorities, Vol II). Since 1920 the German minority in Denmark has remained relatively stable, but the Danish minority in Germany has fluctuated in size. This was especially the case shortly after 1945, when about half of the resident population in the German part of Schleswig sided with the Danish minority and added their claims for some form of autonomy, self government or even joining Denmark.

People who had sympathised with the Danes during the German occupation of Denmark (1940–1945) or had family there, but had not dared to manifest their nationality before, were now unrestricted. Others who disliked Schleswig's connection with Prussia and preferred a somewhat closer relationship with Denmark, or even thought of the old Danish *Gesamtstaat* or self administration, now opted for Denmark; while yet others suffering from material needs and having no hope in a future revived Germany — understandable in the chaos and hopelessness of the time — decided to move towards the relatively intact Danish neighbour, made more attractive still by the Danish government and various interest groups providing the Danish minority with manpower, money and other material goods. There were also those who now preferred to sympathise with the Danes because they were disappointed with Weimarian democracy or had been persecuted during the Nazi dictatorship.

The sudden explosive rise of the Danish minority reached its climex in 1947, when in the first free Land parliament elections the party of the minority obtained 99,500 votes (in 1932–33 comparative figures are 1,511 and 4,658), and raised the question whether this sudden pro-Danish upswing entitled these "new Danes" to claim statutory minority protection, or whether this movement was only a form of political protest. Unfortunately no figures exist to show how many "new Danes" were motivated by which factors, but by combining the decline of Danish votes since 1947 with the reconstruction of West Germany, the conclusion may be drawn that most were protesting, while others remained attracted by the high standard of education, social services and activities, the Danish "way of life" and were thus socialised into the minority.

The situation in Schleswig-Holstein (Schleswig especially had been situated at the periphery, neglected in economic and financial respect by the centre until 1945) was made more serious by more than one million refugees and expellees from Eastern Germany and adjacent areas. They doubled the resident population and — in Danish view — threatened the "national balance" to the benefit of the German side. Denmark and the Danish minority demanded the refugees be sent to other parts of Germany, an action Germany and the Allied authorities were willing to undertake partially, but for practical reasons it was realised very slowly. Schleswig-Holstein lacked economic and financial resources and the integration of the refugees was, one among other urgent tasks, a heavy burden for the country. As the conditions improved (about 1950) some refugees were moved into other regions, but most remained in Schleswig-Holstein where the residents reacted angrily to the privileges and opportunities they felt were given to refugees and expellees by the government.

Both Germans and the Danish minority were combined in acting against the infiltration of their homeland. Conditions in Schleswig-Holstein were so disastrous that it was planned to give up the *Land* status of Schleswig-Holstein and to form a new *Land* perhaps with Hamburg or Lower Saxony to share resources. When these efforts failed there was one alternative: to get money from the Federal government in Bonn derived from the "wealthier" *Lander* for compensation. This was successful and in 1954 Prime Minister Lubke started a large land improvement programme in Schleswig which still continues.

In Denmark, the German occupation and the behaviour of the German minority from 1933 onwards discredited the German minority. "Collaborators" were brought to trial, schools closed, property confiscated, so that it became nearly impossible for the Germans in North Schleswig to maintain the status of a minority. Despite German wishes (1920–24, 1954–55) Denmark has always rejected any kind of binding treaties or agreements relating to international law in connection with the German minority: as a small state Denmark has historical fears that Germany would use such a treaty for interference into internal Danish matters. On the other hand, Denmark largely protected and promoted the inflated Danish minority which German authorities and "national" interest groups in Schleswig-Holstein were reluctant to accept as a genuine minority.

Minority protection in Schleswig is based on an implied reciprocity between both states, without any legal obligations. When the level of conflict is low this principle has turned out to be functional and effective. When in 1949 a declaration of minority rights was negotiated between the Schleswig-Holstein *Land* government and representatives of the Danish minority (under significant participation of British authorities) and approved by the *Land* government, fundamental minority rights were granted under the "Kiel Declaration" of September 1949. The Land government and parliament expected reciprocity from the Danish government, but the Danish Prime Minister only agreed to receive some representatives to read a prepared outline, based on the Protocol of Copenhagen; it was not regarded as equivalent to the Kiel Declaration. The Danish government emphasised that there was no need for special minority rights for the German minority because as Danish citizens they were sufficiently protected. The Germans wanted special affirmative codification of their rights as a minority.

Under the Kiel Declaration, anybody may call himself "Danish" by will and is the most important provision. Worth mentioning also is that Danish schools may receive per pupil up to 80% of the average cost per German elementary school place. The Danish minority was also allowed to seek governmental approval for private secondary schools, but did not make use of this opportunity until 1955 (probably fearing the necessity to adjust their educational system to the German). Furthermore, a proportional German-Danish committee was established to deal with grievances and complaints of the Danish group; it operated quite effectively from 1949 to 1958, when it was dissolved.

From 1947 the Danish minority was represented in the Kiel *Land* Parliament by several members. In 1954 however, due to the massive decline of Danish votes and the existence of the 5% exclusion clause in Schleswig-Holstein election law, the minority lost its parliamentary representation — while the German minority in Denmark had been able to elect one representative to the Danish parliament in 1953 with about a quarter of the total votes cast for the Danish representative in 1954. This development and Danish dissatisfaction with the way German authorities were fulfilling the Kiel Declaration led to a series of new negotiations in Kiel, Bonn and Copenhagen (1954–55), which were also promoted by external necessities related to NATO. It has been to the credit of the Schleswig-Holstein *Land* government that it persists on searching for a solution to meet the wishes and demands of the Danish minority as well as those of the Germans in North Schleswig. Kiel worked systematically towards a 'package' (based on reciprocity) that contained an entire settlement of all existing minority problems on both sides of the border. Since Denmark refused to accept a formal treaty, a pragmatic result has been achieved: both governments in Bonn and Copenhagen submitted unilateral (but almost identical) declarations to their respective parliaments for approval, so that while an international legally binding agreement was avoided, both declarations are politically binding. The Kiel Declaration was made redundant.

The most important provision of the Bonn declaration is the exemption of the Danish minority from the 5% exclusion clause in Schleswig-Holstein, and in 1958 the Danish group regained its parliamentary representation in Kiel; the Copenhagen declaration re-established the right to maintain private secondary schools for the German minority. Some points remained open: the Danes were not willing to make a formal recognition of the border, refused to discuss the treatment of the German minority, and the Danish minority refused to submit a declaration of loyalty. Since the 1960s these points are no longer burning issues, and both declarations indicate that the level of conflict between Germans and Danes had waned, reflecting a change of attitude towards Germany in Danish public opinion. Although several smaller problems have had to be settled and new problems arise steadily, the general settlement has shown itself to be effective.

In 1964, due to a decline in votes, the German minority lost its parliamentary representation; as a substitute, a consultative committee was established giving minority government and parliamentary parties the opportunity to discuss day-to-day problems. A parallel committee was set up in Bonn at the same time, and since 1975 a consultative committee meets twice a year so that financial and cultural matters may also be discussed in the Kiel *Land* parliament on behalf of the German minority.

Co-operating with a Danish party, the Centre Democrats, the German minority was able to send one M.P. to Copenhagen from 1973 until 1979, when the Centre Democrats refused the German candidate on the grounds of his conduct during the Nazi period.

Since 1945 both minorities have been able to build up and maintain — with substantial subsidies and support from both countries — an educational, cultural and social system of celebrated high standard, so that the border region of Schleswig is now relatively rich.

Wilfred Lagler

9 Development? The Kalinga, Bontoc and Isneg of the Philippines

The Chico River Basin Development Project of the National Power Corporation of the Philippines involves the construction of four giant hydro-electric dams in Northern Luzon. These dams would generate a total of 1,010 Megawatts of hydro-electric power annually, which government planners deem crucial:

> "With the energy crisis it became imperative to pursue construction of the Chico River Dams. All together, the dams would be the biggest in Asia, capable of generating power almost equal in value to our $800 million oil imports."

The dams, however, submerge 2,753 hectares of agricultural land, and displace over one thousand tribal Kalinga and Bontoc families from their terraced rice fields and ancestral burial grounds. The construction of the Chico IV dam alone would flood seven villages: Ableg, Cagaluan, Dupag, Tanglag, Mabongtot, Tomiangan, and Bangad. It would also directly affect the means of support of the 300 families of Lubuagan, Dangtalan, Guinaang and Naneng, since they would lose some P.38,250,000 (£2½ m. approx) of rice fields. The economic system of the Kalinga and Bontoc is based on 'rice culture' with which their political, socio-cultural and religious systems naturally intertwine. Displacement thus threatens the disintegration of their indigenous culture, their heritage and identity.

From the first instance of forceful entry into Cagaluan territory in February 1974 by survey teams of the National Power Corporation, the tribal people have made sustained attempts to express their opposition. Five tribal delegations in 1974 failed to gain audience with President Marcos. In May 1976 the 700-man 60th Philippine Constabulary Battalion together with the armed village militia of the Presidential Assistant on National Minorities (PANAMIN) had for its first assignment the setting up of a camp at the Chico IV site. As the soldiers pitched their tents, hundreds of Kalingas gathered round them, the men carrying bolo and knives standing guard while the women dismantled the tents put up by the soldiers.

By June of the same year a petition to the President expressing opposition to the dams and asking help for the preservation of their culture and heritage had been signed by more than 5,000 Kalinga women and men. During the IMF/World Bank Conference in Manila in October 1976, an open letter from both Kalinga and Bontoc was sent to delegates, informing them that the request by the Philippine Government for IMF financing of the dam project would lead to destruction of tribal livelihood and culture. The World Bank Director for Asia replied to them that resettlement requirements would be carefully studied before a final decision was taken. Financing was finally extended by the IMF while resettlement provisions still remained vague and entirely unacceptable to those affected.

A chain of arrests and the detention of over one hundred Kalinga oppositionists, both men and women, started in late 1976. In some confrontations, when male Kalinga or Bontoc failed to drive away an NPC survey team, the initiative was taken by women who, partially disrobed, succeeded on every occasion in forcing a hasty retreat by the unwelcome teams. This is apparently a 'last resort' tactic, only sanctioned by the community when the social order is seriously threatened by outside forces, as in the case of attempts by Spain to bring the Kalinga area under colonial domination four hundred years ago.

The Chico experience might have taught planners that the people directly affected by projects proposed in the name of development, must be consulted from the beginning. The response of Kalingas and Bontocs suggests that inadequate resettlement proposals, rhetorical appeals to national patriotism, military intimidation, and repeated attempts to co-opt traditional leaders by manipulation of their peace-pact systems, have all failed in the face of communal solidarity. By October 1979 construction work on any of the Chico dams had yet to begin.

However, to the North of the Chico project, the NPC is pursuing the implementation of a much larger hydro-electric development in Apayao sub-province, known as the Abulug

project. The First phase, Abulug I at Gened, will flood 9,400
hectares of land in Kabugao municipality and displace at least
850 families, all of whom are Isneg, the major tribe in Apayao.
This figure is an estimate made by the Japanese consultants
(New Japan Engineering Consultants Inc, Osaka). Field reports,
however, indicate that in recent years the Binuan Valley to be
inundated has been subject to considerable inward migration
from Cagayan and Kalinga. The number of families affected,
therefore, is likely to be very much in excess of the official
estimate.

The Isneg live primarily in settlements along the river where
they maintain small plots of land on level ground, planting
tobacco (the chief cash crop), coffee, sugar, corn, vegetables and
some wet rice. Most families however own and operate a *kaingin*
farm in the hills which produces the stable food crops. Collecting
fruits, seeds and roots in the forests, hunting and fishing, and
raising domestic animals supplement the farm produce. Reynolds
and Grant estimate that for every hectare cultivated at any given
time, another ten are laying fallow recuperating their fertility
for future use. The question of resettlement thus becomes
extremely delicate. Available information indicates that one hectare only per household is the recommended resettlement offer
likely to be situated in areas alien to the Isneg traditional
agricultural practices.

At issue is the concept of land ownership, which the Government views very differently from the Isneg:

> "The Philippine Government regards the vast area of Apayao
> as one of its undeveloped, but potentially valuable resources.
> It sees mineral deposits that may produce vast wealth; virgin
> forests; water resources, which can be used for power and
> irrigation; and large tracts of land, which may one day meet
> the needs of land-hungry tenant farmers in the lowlands."

The Isnegs, on the other hand, regard the land as theirs:

> "For hundreds of years, they have lived in Apayao. Every
> hectare of land has belonged to a particular family, whether
> they are farming it that year or letting it lie fallow. Everyone
> knew what property belonged to each family. In former years
> . . . the penalty for trespassing on Isneg land was death."

Conflict, therefore, is a very real possibility. The government views the land as basically free for the taking, but the Isneg can account for every hectare. Add to this the relative secrecy under which the NPC has ordered work to proceed on the Abulug project, and the future for the Isneg is indeed disturbing. A public disclosure of plans and resettlement proposals by the Philippine Government, for full discussion with Isneg representatives, is essential.

Scilla McLean

BIBLIOGRAPHY

Philippine Panorama 13 Nov 1977
Renolds and Grant. *The Isneg of the Northern Luzon, a Study of Trends of Change and Development* 1968
Report on System-wise Optimisation Study August 1978
NEWJEC, Osaka

10 Fiji

The graffiti on the walls of the University of the South Pacific are expressed in language that is as unprintable as the language of graffiti everywhere, but the tenor of the remarks is different. Two views find expression: on the one side it is asserted that unless the immigrant community accepts its position as the labourers working for the indigenous masters, members of the first community can expect an early use to be made of the guns the masters possess; on the other is expressed a despising view of the savage '*Junghs*'. But there is no answer to the argument of the gun. The two communities are those of the Fijians and the Fiji citizens of Indian origin. Which is to be treated as the minority in need of constitutional and political safeguards depends in part on the present and projected population figures (in thousands).

	Chinese		European		Fijian		Indian		Part European		All Other		Total
	No	%	No	%	No	%	No	%	No	%	No	%	
1881 Census	—	—	3	2	115	90	1	1	1	1	8	6	127
1891 Census	—	—	2	2	106	88	7	6	1	1	5	4	121
1901 Census	—	—	2	2	94	78	17	14	2	2	5	4	120
1911 Census	—	—	4	3	87	62	40	29	2	1	7	5	140
1921 Census	1	1	4	2	54	54	61	39	3	2	4	3	157
1936 Census	2	1	4	2	98	50	85	43	5	2	4	2	198
1946 Census	3	1	5	2	118	45	120	46	6	2	8	3	260
1956 Census	4	1	6	2	148	43	169	49	8	2	10	3	345
1966 Census	5	1	7	2	202	42	241	51	10	2	12	3	477
1975 Estimate					252	44	288	51					
1976 Estimate*					269	44.2	293	49.8					

(*In 1976 a Census was conducted, but the findings have not yet been officially published. These figures are rounded up from the figures 259,932 Fijians and 292,896 Indians respectively.)

Thus, for the first time since censuses were conducted, those of Indian origin, as a percentage of the total population, have declined, and they now constitute marginally under 50% of the total population.

This change in the population needs to be explained. From 1881 to 1921 the extensive contact of Fijians with European diseases such as measles and influenza led to a considerable increase in the Fijian death rate so that the Fijian population declined from approximately 115,000 in 1881 to 84,000 in 1921. In this same period between 40,000 and 50,000 Indians arrived in Fiji as indentured labourers or as immigrants. By 1921 sponsored immigration had ceased and the death rate among Fijians decreased. From 1921 to 1956 the important cause of changing population of Fijians and those of Indian origin in the population derived from the birth rate, there being little evidence of differential mortality among the two. The birth rate among those of Indian origin in the period from 1921 to 1956 was 2.94% — a high value which meant that the population size was doubling in less than 24 years. The population growth rate among Fijians, on the other hand was 1.60%. One important factor explaining this difference in birth rates was the different ages at which women married. Among those of Indian origin the average age at marriage in 1921 was 13 years increasing to 17 years in 1956. In the same period the average age of marriage among Fijian women remained stable at 22 years.

In the period since 1956 there has been a significant change in the relative growth rates of the Fijian population and that of Indian origin. There has been a decrease in Indian fertility, with a certain level of economic and social development and the average age of marriage has increased appreciably; births are also concentrated in the early years of marriage and the use of contraceptive methods has increased. With Fijians, on the other hand, the factors which, among those of Indian origin, have worked to reduce the birth rate, have had markely less effect and Fijian fertility is now significantly higher than among those of Indian origin. Focusing on the period 1972–74 where data is provided in the Fiji Fertility Survey, a demographer has recently estimated the difference in total fertility rate as 26%.

There has also been an increase in the rate of emigration of those of Indian origin. Thus over the last five years of colonial rule (1964–69) the average annual net emigration of Fijian citizens of Indian origin was 272: in the first five years after colonial rule (1970–74) the corresponding average was 1,552, more than a fivefold increase.

The effect is that in ten years there will be a change of major importance in the population situation in Fiji: by 1988 Fijians will have overtaken the Fijian citizens of Indian origin as the largest racial group in the population of the country. This has far-reaching implications.

Fiji became independent in 1970 with a constitution that had been developed with explicit reference to the population situation then prevailing and projections on the basis of these figures for the future. The Fijians were the minority and the constitution went out of its way to safeguard their interests. There were five particular forms of such safeguards. First, the legislature was constituted with two houses and in the Senate — which has significant delaying powers — Fijians were in effect guaranteed a majority. The Great Council of Fijian Chiefs was recognised in the constitution and empowered to nominate eight of the twenty two members, and the Council of Rotuma one member; the prime minister was empowered to nominate seven members and the leader of the opposition six. Assuming the Fijian interests dominated either in the government or opposition, Fijian control of the Senate was assured.

Second and more important, the laws safeguarding the whole machinery of separate administration of Fijians, their control over land, the basis for leasing of land to non-Fijians and the administration of Fijian development funds — in other words a major part of the statute law governing Fijians — all this was entrenched in the constitution, and no change could be made in such law except with the agreement of six of the eight Council of Fijian Chiefs' representatives in the Senate. Third, the House of Representatives was to be elected using a complex method of communal representation. This provided for an equal number of representatives chosen separately by Indians and Fijians and again equal numbers of each race chosen by all the electors of the separate constituencies. Representatives of the other racial communities acting under the label of "general electors" then held the balance of the seats. This electoral system ensured that Fijians would be assured close to half the seats in the lower house. The remaining two provisions were of more limited significance. The constitution did, however, provide as a fundamental right that the individual should be protected from discrimination on the grounds of race but this did not apply to existing law. Thus it could apply to existing discriminatory law in favour of Fijians but could prevent discrimination against them for the future. Finally, it was provided that the Public Service Commission in recruiting to the public service was to ensure that each community in Fiji received fair treatment in the number and distribution of appointments.

One provision was notable by its absence; there was no mention in the constitution of how the army was to be controlled nor of how the army was to be composed. There was nothing, for instance, that was parallel to the stipulation concerning the public service that each community should receive fair treatment. In fact the army was almost totally Fijian. Citizens of Indian origin having refused to join the army in World War II unless paid at the same rate as European recruits, the army was retained as a Fijian preserve and nothing was done in the transfer of power from the British, either in the constitution or otherwise, to change this.

Within the limits of the stated safeguards for the Fijian minority — and the unstated but recognised safeguard provided by the army — the constitution assumed the operation of representative and responsible government using the Westminster model. The way electoral politics has worked under this constitution, one party — the Alliance Party — has retained office since independence in 1970. This party is an alliance of three racial associations — a Fijian association dominated by the Fijian Chiefs and operating through the separate official machinery of Fijian administration (to the extent, for instance, of vehicles of the Native Land Trust Board being used as Alliance Party vehicles in the election campaigns in 1977) an associated of General Electors, and the Indian Alliance. The Fijian association has been the dominant partner; and the Indian Alliance the weakest, the major support of those of Indian origin going to the second main party, the National Federation Party. Nevertheless, the existence of the Indian Alliance proved sufficient up to 1977 to split the Indian vote and to allow a monolithic Fijian vote, allied with the general electors to ensure a majority for the Alliance. Throughout this party Fijians, and particularly Fijian chiefs were able to be the dominant influence in government.

In a general election in March 1977, however, the dominance of the Alliance Party and of Fijian chiefs was questioned. In this election for the first time the Fijian Association within the Alliance was challenged among Fijian voters by a new party — the Fiji National Party — which was both more militant in its claims for Fijians as against Indians, and at the same time represented common interests among Fijians against the Fijian chiefs. The presence of this party split the Fijian vote in several constituencies. At the same time were was a marked decline in electoral support for the Indian Alliance associated with the reaction against the overt discrimination against citizens of Indian origin in the award of entrance scholarships to University, the one national issue in the election campaign. In the result the Alliance Party was reduced to being the minority party in the House of Representatives, having twenty four seats to the National Federation Party's twenty six, with one independent associated loosely with the NFP, and one representative of the Fiji National Party who was actively opposed to both the Alliance Party and the NFP. In the result the Governor General — a senior Fijian chief and former Alliance Party politician, reappointed Ratu Mara the leader of the Alliance Party as Prime Minister. In doing so the Governor General reinterpreted the precisely expressed guidance in the constitution on who was to be appointed Prime Minister, and ignored the convention which elsewhere in the Commonwealth are taken to apply in the circumstances in which the Governor General found himself. When the majority in the House of Representatives passed a resolution requesting the Governor General to appoint as Prime Minister the leader of the majority party, the Governor General kept strictly to the provisions of the constitution and granted the Prime Minister a further dissolution.

In the ensuing election in September 1977 the Alliance Party returned with a clear majority so vindicating, in the view of some, the action of the Governor General. The result, however, derived primarily from a division in the National Federation Party, which resulted in a measure caused by the failure of the Governor General's actions. It was also notable however, that the Alliance Party made ready use of the machinery of the state and the Fijian administration to secure an Alliance Party election victory.

The constitutional crisis of 1977 encouraged disillusionment with the existing constitution among Fiji citizens of Indian descent. This is reflected most evidently in the demands for reforms in the constitution. There has been a realisation that the constitution can be operated to exclude Fiji citizens of Indian descent from an effective share of power. Moreover much as this community wishes to break through the rigid boundaries set by the state around the different racial communities — and allow at this level for the relatively harmonious and cooperative relationships that exist at the grass roots — the Alliance Party government, reflecting in particular the interests of the Fijian chiefs, is reinforcing those boundaries, using a generalised threat of Indian domination as the justification for strengthening the control of Fijian chiefs.

Meanwhile the dominant position in government occupied by the Fijians and particularly the Fijian chiefs is adding further to the disadvantages felt by Fijian citizens of Indian descent. In public service recruitment for example each community is required to receive fair treatment. In the public service (using 1977 figures) and taking only posts filled by Fiji citizens, 44% of these posts are filled by Indians; 50% by Fijians. More strikingly, taking all the top policy making posts in ministerial departments and para-governmental bodies (using 1978 figures), 45% of the posts are filled by Fijians, 41% by expatriates, Europeans and others and 13% by Indians. Where, at independence in 1970, half the permanent secretaries were of Indian origin, now the score is nine Fijian, three Indian. Yet in admission to University and medical school, Fijians are still given preferential treatment on account of the supposed backwardness of this community relative to the Indian community.

The Fiji citizens of Indian origin have been a disadvantaged community. At the time when Fiji became independent, this community accepted the position with some expressed hesitations. This was done in the belief that the working of the Westminster model constitution, combined with their majority position in the population, would mean that over time the extent of the discrimination against them would be moderated. The years 1977 and 1978 have brought out the weakness of their situation. Fijian citizens of Indian origin are extensively discriminated against, and the constitutional crisis of 1977 showed how little faith could be placed in the constitution. Now the results of the 1976 census and the projections based on it show that this community is on the way to becoming not only one with minority constitutional and political rights, but a numerical minority as well. In the meantime the Australians have equipped the Fijian dominated army with automatic rifles as a replacement for the less efficient 303s.

David Murray

BIBLIOGRAPHY

Hoefnagel, E.R., *The Demographic Situation in Fiji*, cyclostyled paper, University of the South Pacific, 1977
Murray, D.J., "The Fiji Constitutional Crisis" 1977, in *Politics*, 1978

11   The Greeks in Albania

Albania, the most secret of all Balkan countries, also has its minorities: tiny fragmented communities of Vlachs, Gypsies, Bulgarians, Serbs and Montenegrins. However the largest and most conspicuous are the Greeks in the southern provinces, along the Greek-Albanian border and in and around the towns of Korçe and Gjinokaster. This area — Northern Epirus to the Greeks — has long been a pawn in Balkan chessboard diplomacy, to the misfortune of its inhabitants.

In the early 1970s, the Greek-speaking community numbered between 50,000 and 72,000 people. The Albanian-Greeks are traditionally a trading and industrial community, although some are farmers in the rich valleys of the south. Having been bargained away during the wars of the early 20th century, their current problems are largely the result of the Hoxha government's policies against the Orthodox church and against Greek-language schools. The Albanian language is unrelated to any other in Europe, although there have been some Slav admixtures. Albania was a region rather than a nation, divided mainly between two groups, the mountain-dwelling Ghegs in the north, and the Tosks, tenant farmers in the south.

In classical times, the Hellenisation of what is today the northwestern frontier area of Greece, was delayed by the region's arid climate and rugged terrain. The Greeks called the region "Epiros", a word with no precise English equivalent but meaning vast, uncivilised and uncongenial. The Greeks nevertheless extended trading colonies, and during early Christian times, monasteries and farming communities. Under 500 years of Turkish rule, which reached up the Balkans almost as far as Vienna, Greek culture and Orthodox Christianity were replaced by Islam. The Turks favoured the Albanians over the Greeks, but even under Turkish rule the province Epiros round Ioannina which then included southern Albania, was designated a Greek-speaking province by Ali Pasha. In the early 19th century further Greek migration into southern Albania took place as Greece became politically independent. The new Greek government, backed by the Western Powers, laid claim to most of southern Albania. Albania itself was formed in 1912, and in 1913 Greece expressed a claim to all Albanian territory south of a line drawn from Vlore on the coast to the southern end of Lake Ochrid, about one third of present Albanian territory, but the International Boundary Commission confirmed the present border on the basis of majority settlement.

In 1924, an able and unscrupulous tribal leader from the north, Ahmed Zog, seized power, with assistance from Yugoslavia. Zog turned to Italy for assistance later to counterbalance Yugoslav influence. The Greeks unsuccessfully invaded Albania during what became a de facto pro-Italian protectorate in the late 1930s, and revitalised their claim. In the morass after World War II, Albania, like other Balkan countries, turned Communist — a reaction against foreign and particularly Italian domination and facism. Seeking Soviet support to prevent Yugoslav incursion, and later Chinese aid to offset Soviet influence, Albania looked inward to effect rapid social change. The tribal conservative northerners still had strong kinship ties, fierce blood feuds, and rigid marriage customs, which the new government was anxious to reduce. Orthodox Christianity, which is also conservative, represented another binding loyalty that could split the unity of state. Suspicions too that the Greeks would always look southward were to dominate the new government's thinking. Greece was prevented from going Communist by the Allies, and now has the extremes of wealth and poverty (the former perhaps an attractive illusion to Albanian Greeks).

Relations between Greece and Albania deteriorated completely with the Corfu Channel incident and Albanian involvement in the Greek Civil War. As the Communists were losing in Greece many fled to Albania taking hostages to ensure their safe passage. Albania was later accused of kidnapping children. 123 Greek hostages, along with several thousand head of cattle and sheep were repatriated to Greece in December 1961. Since then, after several trade agreements and treaties, the Greek government has largely abandoned their claim to "Northern Epirus". This improvement in Albanian/Greek relations has now denied the Greeks of southern Albania an extra-territorial champion to seek redress for educational and religious grievances.

In the southern Albanian province, Chamuria, the state schools are Albanian, although the Greek community have been able to maintain their own. Albanian governments, both before and since World War II, have tried to extend Albanian cultural influence into the Greek areas. In 1935 the Hague Tribunal prevented the Zog government from dissolving the Greek-language schools, and the Hoxha government has pledged support for the schools, while at the same time severely limiting the use of Greek, preventing new schools from being established and closing down all churches. The elimination of religion is an essential element of Hoxha's

policies and throughout the whole of Albania religious activities
are reported to have been banned.

Randall Fegley

BIBLIOGRAPHY

Marmullaku, R., *Albania and the Albanians*, London, 1975
Papadakis, V.P., *Histoire Diplomatique de la Question Nord-
Epirote*, Athens, 1958
Pipinelis, P., *Europe and the Albanian Question*, Chicago, 1963
Skendi, S., *Albania*, New York, 1956
Wolff, R.L., *The Balkans in Our Time*, Cambridge, Mass, 1974
Xydis, S.G., *Greece and the Great Powers*, Thessaloniki, 1963

12   The Greenlanders

Greenland is the world's biggest island, with a total area of
8,400,000 square miles, of which about 93% is covered to a depth
of 10,000 feet by the Arctic ice. Although it is 2,500 miles away
from Denmark, and fifty times larger, the island has been an
integral part of Denmark since 1953, when its colonial status
was abolished. It has magnificent scenery with fjords and glaciers
among the most impressive in the world, air free from pollution,
temperatures falling regularly to −70° C, a rich fauna, a coast-
line of 24,000 miles and a population of 47,935 (1972).

All Greenlanders are Danish citizens but only about 8,000 are
of completely European stock; the rest are Eskimos who are of
mixed Danish, Norwegian and Viking descent but who, for the
most part, are ethnically akin to the other peoples of Northern
Canada, Alaska and Siberia. These Eskimos speak *Kalatdisu* a
holophrastic or polysynthetic speech, rich in vocabulary for use
in its own community and essential to their culture, but not yet

wholly adapted for use in the world beyond. Greenland is known to the Eskimos as *Kalatdlit Nunat* — the Land of Men.

The island was first visited by Europeans when Eric the Red visited it around the year A.D. 960. He persuaded about 3,000 of his Icelandic compatriots to settle in Greenland, inventing the name to attract them to what is still one of the bleakest territories inhabited by man. In 1270, the Norsemen of Greenland hoped to improve their economy, which had declined after Europe lost interest in the narwhale tusks which they had supplied, and some swore fealty to Norway, allowing Norwegians a trade monopoly. Early contacts with the Eskimos were hostile: in the fourteenth century the West Settlement was destroyed by the Eskimos and the East Settlement attacked. By the year 1500 communications with Norway had ceased and when, over two hundred years later, the Norwegian missionary Hans Egede (1686–1758) went to preach the Lutheran faith in Greenland, isolated since before the Reformation, he found only the ruins of the Norsemen's settlement. Whether malnutrition, disease, a deterioration of the climate, the effects of constant inter-marriage or attacks by Eskimos had wiped them out is not known; their fate remains one of the great unsolved mysteries of the Middle Ages.

Up to this time the Eskimos had depended on a natural economy based on seal-hunting which provided them with all their needs. But during the eighteenth and nineteenth centuries Denmark began trade with Greenland, mainly for cryolite, a component of aluminium which the island had in plentiful supply. The Eskimos responded to these new contacts by bartering animal-skins in exchange for the cargoes of European sugar, and coffee especially, to such an extent that there was soon a severe food shortage in the island. The Danes introduced the Greenland trade monopoly, to protect their own interests and to shield the Eskimos from further exploitation; it was a paternalistic act but genuinely humanitarian: as early as the eighteenth century they saw their duty to protect the ethnic identity of the Eskimos.

A period of stagnation during the nineteenth century was largely the result of a decline in the seal-catch following the arrival of European sealers off the coast of Newfoundland. The population increased from about 7,000 in 1834 to 9,000 in 1855. The man responsible for tackling the island's problems in the face of diminishing interest on the part of the Danish government was H.J. Rink (1819–1893) who, as Director of the Greenland

Trade Organisation from 1871-1882, was charged with carrying
out Danish policy in their colony. He was exceptional in his
encouragement for Eskimo culture, including the publication of
a magazine. At first, efforts to encourage the Greenlanders to
participate in the administration of their island met with little
success, but after 1901 a new organisation known as the Danish
Atlantic Islands began to make headway; seven years later a law
was passed which introduced local councils and a National
Council, elected by all the island's inhabitants, but still under
the jurisdiction of the Danish Government.

Around 1917, following an increase in temperature, large
quantities of cod arrived in Greenland's waters and there was a
switch from sealing to fishing, depots being built for salting the
catch. With this revival of trade, the Eskimos could now import
European foods, and sheep-farming was also established. In the
years between the two World Wars, Greenland was treated by
the Danish Government as a closed territory — once again on
the ground that a unique ethnic group would suffer if exposed
to the impact of the industrial world. Outsiders, including Danes,
were not admitted except by special permission from the Greenland Board in Copenhagen, and little was heard about the island.
Highly skilled practitioners in the art of survival in one of the
world's most atrocious climates — the world learned about the
inhabitants only from films like Robert Flaherty's *Nanook of the
North* (1922).

The twentieth century began in Greenland in 1940 when the
Americans started building their air-fields, intermediate stops on
the way to the battle-fields of Europe, and as part of the defences
of the United States against the threat of German attack. Although
contacts between Eskimos and Americans was at first sporadic,
the Greenlanders — cut off from occupied Denmark — soon
became dependent on food supplies from the U.S.A. and familiar
with a new standard of living. As a result, the windows were
swung open so wide that they could never again be closed. After
the War prominent Greenlanders declared in the United Nations
that they wished to remain attached to Denmark but that the old
colonialism, the trade monopoly and the isolation must end. In
1953, following the report of the Greenland Commission, the
island was granted the status of a Danish *Amt* (county), a
provincial council was elected under a Governor, and Greenland
was given direct representation in the *Folketing* in Copenhagen.

These reforms were accompanied by strenuous attempts to improve living conditions for the Eskimos. The health service was extended in a bid to combat the widespread incidence of tuberculosis, infant mortality, alcoholism and syphilitic diseases. The population increased from 21,000 in 1956 to 30,000 in 1960 and to 45,000 in 1968. Massive investment by Denmark brought materials and labour for the construction of homes, schools, hospitals, power-stations and factories — in short, for the first time, the entire infrastructure for sustaining a modern, urban population. Education similar to that available in Denmark was introduced in 1956, pride of place being given to the teaching of Danish. Such progress brought its own problems, of course, not least being the devastating effects of the traditional culture of the Eskimos. Hans Egede and H.J. Rink had admired their distinctive way of life, but most of those who came after believed the Eskimos to be without culture.

The artistic creativity of the hunter was the first to decline. The legends preserved in oral tradition were replaced by Danish folk-tales, the music by hymn-singing and the composition of poetry also declined. There was a reaction against the process of Danicisation during the 1960s, and a balance between the language in the schools has still not been achieved, although both languages are taught at primary and secondary level; there is no university in Greenland. Apart from the small number of Danes who learn Greenlandic, only the younger generation of Eskimos is bilingual. The debate over language over the last two decades must be seen in the context of a growing national awareness among the Eskimos and in particular, of the younger generation's search for a new identity. There are still Eskimos who live in the north-west and east of the island, a few of the island families depending on seals, whales, polar bears, foxes, reindeer and birds, and only to a small extent on the products of a new age. Most of Greenland's population is concentrated in about 120 settlements and 20 small townships which include Frederikshåb, Sukkertoppen, Holsteinborg and Godthåb (pop. 7,600 in 1972), the capital.

Among the young Greenlanders' criticisms of Danish policies in the island was the belief that it was a mistake to base Greenland's development on the Danish patterns, that Greenlanders cannot be expected always to behave like Danes, and that they must be given a greater degree of autonomy in their own affairs. The Danish Government responded to this criticism in 1975 by asking Isi Foighel, professor of international law at Copenhagen University, to consider a new, self-governing status for Greenland. It was this Commission's proposals to the Danish Government which were the subject of the referendum held in Greenland in January 1979. By a vote of 70% in favour and 25.8% against, the islanders opted for self-government.

This convincing vote was welcomed by Copenhagen and greeted in Greenland as a victory for the political parties, *Atasut* and *Siumut*, which had campaigned for the establishment of a Greenlandic Parliament during the past six years. These two parties also won a majority of the 21 seats in the election to the *Landsting*, Greenland's new Parliament, which took place on 4 April 1979. This body took over responsibility for industry, education, taxation and cultural affairs from the disbanded Provincial Council; defence and foreign policy remain under Danish control. There seems to be no question of Greenland's withdrawing from the Danish State: the measure of autonomy won by its people is similar to that of the Faroe Islands.

During the past thirty years Denmark has put more into Greenland than it has taken out. Far from being self-supporting, the island receives annual grants from metropolitan Denmark of about 1,000 million kroner, but exports amount to about half that sum and consist largely of lead and zinc from the Black Angel mines in the north of the island. Denmark's attempts to modernise life in Greenland have been of unique dimensions. What is not yet clear is whether a European community can be maintained in extreme Arctic conditions among a people who are not, after all, European. What has taken place in Greenland since 1945 is in every respect a break with the past, the Danish Government compressing into decades the development elsewhere in centuries. But the questions arising from the new situation are now for the Greenlanders themselves to answer.

Meic Stephens

BIBLIOGRAPHY

Berthelsen, C., *Development of the Educational System in Greenland 1950–1970*. Copenhagen, 1971
Dyssegard, S., *Greenland Arctic Denmark*, Copenhagen, 1970

Erngaard, Erik, *Greenland, Then and Now*, New York, 1972
Hammerick, L.L., *The Eskimo Language*, Oslo, 1969
Rink, H.J., *Danish Greenland*, London, 1974
Rink, H.J., *Tales and Traditions of the Eskimo*, London, 1975

13 Iran: Two Revolutions and Iranian Minorities

Minorities in Iran may be divided into the tribes of Iranian origin and major groups speaking Turkic, Arabic and other languages. Towards the end of the nineteenth century the proportion of the tribal population to the whole was about one third, some 2 million out of 7 million. Now the remaining nomadic tribes constitute about one seventeenth, some 2 million out of 34 million. The Shah's policy, once a settled way of life had been largely imposed, was the spread of literacy and culture, and the compulsory use of standard *Farsi* (Persian) in education. The Ministry of Education's Tribal Education Centre and the revolutionary corps, combined with increasing employment of tribal youth in industry, agriculture and services had begun to dissolve the tribal structure in Iran generally.

Of the larger groups speaking Iranian (Indo-European in origin) languages, there are about 3.5 million *Kurds* constituting a third of the world's Kurdish population. They are to be found in Kurdistan, Western Azerbaijan and Kermanshahan on the north western borders with Iraq and Turkey. 90% of the Kurds now live in towns or villages. There are even more *Luri* speakers than Kurds, living in Western Iran; over half are now sedentary. Other smaller groups speaking Iranian languages are the *Hezareh, Barberi, Teimuri, Jamshidi* and the *Afghans* in Khorasan, the *Quadikolahi* and *Palavi* in Mazandaran and the *Sanani* and *Agajani* in Talesh.

Half a million *Bakhtiari* travel across the Zagros mountains annually, wintering in Khuzestan, where they grow wheat and

barley. Traditionally hostile, they are divided into several sub-
tribes — *taifeh*. The basic unit is the camp, the *mal*, of a half a
dozen tents. They follow traditional routes herding sheep and
goats and travelling on ponies. They wear distinctive clothing
with black domed hats for the men. Camp work is divided
between the sexes — Bakhtiari women do not wear the veil and
are more free socially than those of many other groups in Iran.
About 1 million *Baluchis* live in the south-east, remote from
Tehran and Afghanistan. They generally rely on a mixture of
nomadic pastoralism and settled agriculture. They have small
agricultural plots which, under customary law, must be regularly
tended by their owners or forfeit. Baluch society is strongly
hierarchical; its remoteness has given it a sense of independence
now coming into conflict with the extension of roads and thereby
of government. Unlike the majority of Iranians, whether tribal
or sedentary, they are not Shi'ia Moslems, but Sunni.

The Turkic speaking tribes of Iran include the *Turkmens* (see
volume 2) and the *Sahsavans* and *Afshar* who inhabit the foothills
of Sabalan mountains in east Azerbaijan on the Soviet border in
summer and Dasht Mogan in winter. This semi-nomadic pattern
is shared by the *Qashqai*, numbering some 150,000 who go up
into the highlands near Seminon, north-west of Isfahan in summer from the drier lands south-east of Shiraz where they winter.
Other Turkic speakers include the 5 *Khamseh* tribes who migrate
between Darab and Lar in eastern Fars, and constitute a mixture
of Arab, Turk and Lur, and other smaller tribes such as the
Qajar, Qara, Goqlu, Moqaddam, Teimurtash and *Bayat*.

According to the 1966 census there were about 380,000 Arabic
speaking people in Iran. Most are settled in Khuzestan, southern
Fars and along the Persian Gulf, where the oil installations are
to be found. There are some 30,000 Gypsies around Shiraz,
Hamadan, Arak, Nahavand, Borujard and Tehran.

During the middle ages nomadic incursions may have caused
an actual decline in sedentary settlement patterns existing since
prehistoric times, but the advent of the Arabs in the seventh
century with the Islamic faith probably encouraged urbanisation.
Tenth century Arab geographers described the Kurds as the
principal nomads; they have been in the area since prehistoric
times. Later Turkmen and Tartars seized vast tracts of land.
These invasions drove the Baluchis south into Kirman and later
east into the Sistan and the Makran where they absorbed the

Dravidian population. The Qashqai are first mentioned in 1415, and they, like the Bakhtiari, formed themselves into confederations during the seventeenth century. Later the Bakhtiari leaders became local tax collectors for the central government. The Qavan family of Shiraz organised the Khamseh confederation to protect caravans and balance Qashqai power in the middle of the nineteenth century. The Qajar organised the Teke Turcomen. From Mongol times until Reza Shah came to power in 1925, Iran was ruled by dynasties of tribal origin, ensuring that tribal support was integral part of the power structure.

Under Reza Shah Pahlavi, brigandage was largely stamped out and seasonal migration was prevented. Huts replaced tents, but as refuse — no longer abandoned en route — accumulated so disease increased. In 1932 state lands were allocated to the tribes but the army and police officials assigned to introduce the changes were known to use threats of force and not all the funds voted for the tribes reached their destination. Some tribesmen were forced to purchase land which had been allocated to them free. Tribal leaders were obliged to live in Tehran. In August 1941 the tribes rebelled and destroyed the settlements. Reza Shah abdicated shortly afterwards and left Iran, war had intervened, and the country was in turmoil (see volume 2, Turkmens). In 1951 the young Shah's second but childless marriage with Soraya, daughter of a leading family of the Bakhtiari tribe, helped to win the latter's support. From 1957 the Shah revived his father's policy of enforced settlement. After a land reform official was shot in Qashqai country in November 1962 and with some evidence of rebellion in March 1963, an attack was mounted on the southern tribes. The Boi Ahmadi were even bombed from the air.

Shia Islam was made the state religion of Iran under the Safavids in 1501. Under the Shah, the constitution recognised Christianity, Zoroastrianism and Judaism as minority religions, but not the Bahai sect which constitutes the largest religious minority. Within Islam there are also Ismailis and Sufis, and the Kurd, Baluch and Turkmen belong to the Sunni faith. Jewish quarters survive in the cities such as Shiraz, Tehran and Mashbad. About 10,000 Zoroastrians remain holding the pre-Islamic faith of Iran. At Kirman, after religious riots, the Zoroastrians largely abandoned their old quarter to the Moslems, some migrating to Tehran, others leaving the country altogether. The

Armenian Christians, also in the north, lived in a state of constant friction with the Kurds. Hebrew and Armenian literature could be published and the Armenians, Assyrians, Jews and Zoroastrians were represented by elected deputies in the *Majlis* (parliament); communications were improved to further this policy. These uneasy tolerances have now changed.

The Shah's revolution in government was applied to all areas of Iran. Land reform was partially completed by 1971. Previously, ownership of villages had fallen into 3 categories, the royal Pahlavi lands — many of them acquired by the Shah's father — the private secular and religious estates, and the *Khaleseh* or public domain. The distribution of land in Khaleseh villages began in 1958. Of 1,536 such villages distributed by June 1970, 1,421 lay in Azerbaijan, Kermanshahan, Khuzestan and Fars. The reform of private lands from 1962 proceeded at first most quickly in Khorasan, and slowly in the Tehran area, but hardly at all in Yazd and Baluchistan. There were difficulties amongst illiterate cultivators (for example in Yazd), with the distinction between custom and contract. The alternatives between landholding by the division of the harvest under custom (usually a fifth), joint working of the land in a communal enterprise, outright sale or a thirty year lease or, indeed the possibility of the landlord buying out the tenants' interests, created confusion. By 1971, however, 800,000 tenants had benefited from division or sale from 260,000 landlords throughout the country.

Other aspects of the Revolution also benefited the economically backward areas. For example a period of teaching in remote areas was made an alternative to military service for university graduates. Teachers were also recruited from amongst the tribesmen. There were about 300,000 tribesmen in Fars province who were almost totally illiterate until Mohammed Bahmenbegin's education programme began in 1952. Then 30,000 children started attending mobile tent-schools for 9 months of the year.

Azerbaijan is a rich and fertile area and has a tradition of independence. Under the Shah, Azeri, a Turkic language, although in daily use, was not permitted for publications because Farsi was to be generally promoted for written communication. The frontier between Iranian and Russian Azerbaijan was established in the early nineteenth century. Attempts at secession have always involved links with the north east rather than with Turkey. There are also Armenians in both parts of Azerbaijan.

A Bolshevik republic of Gilan was set up to the south east of Azerbaijan in 1921 and survived for a year. Again in 1943, Azerbaijan returned members of the Communist *Tudeh* party to the *Majlis*, and by 1945 the Democratic Party had emerged. Soviet influence was behind the separatist insurrection of November 1945; the rebel government introduced some social and administrative reform. The prospect of an oil agreement with Iran was introduced to persuade the Soviets to withdraw, and for some years after the brutal suppression of the revolt, public services were neglected in the region. Tabriz, the chief city of Azerbaijan and historically an important strategic, commercial and political centre — and at times the capital — has received relatively little state investment in industry and its commercial expansion has been limited with the growth of Tehran and the southern oilfields. It is in Azerbaijan that opposition to Khomeini is now developing.

Kurdish aspirations towards independence have been encouraged both by Soviet influence and by contact with their compatriots in Iraq, Turkey and Syria. Soviets were set up in Kurdish areas of Iran in 1905 and 1918. From 1941 Kurdish areas were within the Soviet occupied zone and in 1945 the Republic of Mahabad was established. The suppression was thorough and many Kurds have since been imprisoned for nationalist ideals. There were short Kurdish language programmes daily on radio and television under the Shah but Kurdish could not be taught in schools. In 1975, Iran's (and the CIA's) military support for the Kurdish rebellion against Iraq's Soviet-backed regime ended with the Algiers Accord, and was regarded as a great betrayal. The Algiers Accord also ended Iraqi support for Arab independence in Khuzestan, another simmering issue for Iran's new government.

Opposition to the Shah mounted with political repression. The press had little freedom. The Shah admitted that there were 3,000 political prisoners, while foreign journalists and Iranian exiles have estimated the number at between 25,000 and 100,000. Torture was widely practised and the secret police, SAVAK, infiltrated every level of society. Any opposition to the monarchy was construed as a crime. Judicial execution was common and not confined to drug-smugglers and terrorists. Trade Unions were illegal. It was thus difficult to distinguish between the

general atmosphere of repression and the suppression of
minorities.

There is widespread ethnic prejudice, particularly in industry.
Afghans provided cheap labour in the south at such projects as
the Chah Bahar oil installations, the Arabs in the Khuzestan oil
fields where the administrative posts tended to be in Persian
hands, and unskilled Azeris used in Tehran seasonal building
trade or the Caspian coal fields.

Although Iran claimed 1,000 years of integral independent
monarchy, her minorities span the boundaries of all her neighbours, and like the Arabs, Kurds and Azeris in the West, the
Afghans and Baluchis along the eastern border are aware of
developments amongst their compatriots under the new regimes
in Afghanistan and in General Zia's Pakistan.

Since the proclamation of the Ayatollah Khomeini's government in 1979, the Arabs, Kurds, Azeris, Turkmen and Baluchis
have all put forward programmes for partial autonomy, and
there has been sporadic violence between them and the Iranian
forces of the revolutionary government. In March 1979, Arab
leaders at an Abadan demonstration demanded a greater share
of Khuzestan's oil revenue, more Arabs in local administrative
and military appointments and the teaching of Arabic as the first
language in schools. Also in March 1979, the Kurds were allowed
a seven-point plan for limited autonomy and a Kurdish governor-
general, but violence has continued. Seizure of the American
Embassy overshadowed rebellions in the regions but fighting has
increased in the Kurdish areas and Azerbaijan. The removal of
law enforcement from the secular courts to revolutionary courts
administrating the *Sharia* or Koranic law, the government's view
of women, and the lack of any concessions to the often regionally
based left-wing and workers' groups which participated in the
Shah's overthrow, would appear to pose a threat to both individual
and minority rights.

An important part of the survival of the Khomeini regime will
be concerned with regional autonomy. Disaffected minorities,
particularly with territories contiguous to other unfriendly countries, can be a continuous source of opposition and insecurity.
Within the cities, the Islamic revolution has taken a repressive
attitude towards the Bahais and Jews. The former, who believe
in a prophet later than Mohammed, are thus deemed to blas-
pheme. There have been anti-Bahai riots before (notably 1955)

but recent inflammatory speeches have encouraged attacks on Bahai owned businesses and banks. The Jews, traditionally less harassed in Iran than elsewhere in the Middle East, have been subject to overt attacks, although only one has been executed, and despite state friendship with the Palestinians, emphatically not as an "agent of Zionism".

The revolution is intended to favour the majority, devout Shi'ia believers, at the expense of the middle class, to which Jews and Bahais belong, along with the new educated oil rich Iranians. The toll has been from among the Shah's appointees to both military and civil service, many acknowledged as corrupt. Nevertheless it is still a sour victory to those who hoped Iran would be free from superstition and coercion.

R.H.

BIBLIOGRAPHY

Ashworth, Georgina, (ed), *World Minorities Vol 2*, London, 1977
Short, Martin & McDermott, Anthony, *The Kurds*, Minority Rights Group, London, 1975

14   Israeli Arabs

There are three major ethnic groups in Israel today: the Ashkenazi Jews of European origin, the Sephardic (Oriental) Jews of Middle Eastern or North African origin and the Arabs who remained within the boundaries of Israel-proper after the 1948 War which brought Israel to statehood. While there are limited parallels between the experience of Oriental Jews and Israeli Arabs, no adequate analogy can be made between the two groups. The Sephardim, as Jews, have eventually been assimilated into Israeli society; the Arabs, as non-Jews, will never have this option. Thus the pre-eminent and problematic cleavage in Israeli society divides Israeli Arabs from Israeli Jews. In 1979 Israeli Arabs were close to 16% of the population: two thirds of these are Moslem, the remainder Christian.

An understanding of Israeli society and politics necessarily entails an acknowledgement of the pervasive infusion of Zionist ideology throughout Israel. The Jewish socialist-pioneering credo of the late nineteenth century (Zionism) is endemic to the institutional structure of the State and is the major facilitator of social cohesion among the ethnically diverse Jewish population. Inherent in this notion is another which ultimately threatens its hegemony: the inability, on the part of Israeli Jews, to consider Israeli Arabs full and equal partners of citizenship. Conversely, the ideology is meaningless, in any positive sense, to the Arab community within Israel.

Zionist ideology, which for Jews represents the "right way of life" is, on a personal level, at best empty and at worst threatening to Israel's Arabs. On a sectarian level it all but disenfranchises Arabs from the State. Zionism is synonymous with Jewish sovereignty. Since the late nineteenth century it has been the shibboleth of generations of pioneers returning to Zion to build a Jewish state. It became an ethic which, by its constant invocation, was infused and institutionalised in all the functions of the State.

The routinisation of Zionist ideology is typified by the party system in Israel. Political parties are multifunctional. They sponsor their own newspapers, publishing houses, youth groups, housing projects and schools, all aligned with the party's particular philosophy. In 1977 there were twenty-two different political parties in Israel, each with its own political line and bait. Nevertheless, Zionism is axiomatic to all of the parties. Any party which is expressly anti-Zionist is banned by law.

Israeli Arabs can participate in mainstream Israeli politics in two ways, each unsatisfying and largely ineffectual: through association with a major Zionist party or through affiliation with the Communist Party. The major parties circulate supplemented Arab lists along with regular party lists. Since election is proportional to the votes received and the lists are ranked according to party seniority, the Arabs have little chance of election. In the past the lists have been used to woo Arab votes without any regard for the welfare of the Arab community.

The Communist Party has been the most potent advocate of Israeli Arab grievances, but even here their voice has not been too effective. Despite its continued support from the Israeli Arab community, the Communist Party has never been included in a government coalition. Nor can its MK's (Members of the Knesset) serve on parliamentary committees which deal with topics which have been deemed "national security areas", since they themselves have been ruled "national security risks".

There have been sporadic attempts by Arabs to form their own political parties. All but one have failed. That one, *al-Ard* (The Land) was outlawed by the Israeli Supreme Court because it was declared to be "basically opposed to the existence of the State of Israel".

The lack of adequate Arab parliamentary representation has abetted the persistent socio-economic gap between Israeli Jews and Arabs. Although their position has risen considerably since statehood due to the large sums of money spent by the government on Arab development, Israeli Arabs still have a lower educational attainment record, a lower overall job status and, not surprisingly, a significantly lower income level than their Jewish counterparts. Arab education has suffered through a policy of separate but equal sectarian schools. There are, in Israel, schools which follow an Arabic curriculum and schools which follow a Jewish curriculum. A recent government survey has found that the Arab schools lack classrooms, trained teachers and textbooks. Over half of the Arab secondary school students fail their matriculation examinations. And less than 3% of all Israeli university students are Arab.

Substandard education has impeded the growth of an Israeli Arab intelligentsia. It has also helped maintain Israeli Arabs at the lowest end of the occupational spectrum. They are concentrated in the unskilled sector as agricultural workers, miners and construction workers. Even when they are qualified, Israeli Arabs are often denied higher paying professional or technical jobs, again in the interests of national security.

Most Israeli Arabs live beyond the cities in essentially self-contained villages, near the borders with Syria, Lebanon and Jordan. More than half the Arab population in the state live in Galilee. The remaining Israeli Arabs reside in the Little Triangle area and the towns near Haifa and the Negev (they are mainly of Bedouin origin). While Israel is highly urbanized, 75% of its Arab population lives in rural locales.

The Israeli Government has perceived these Arab enclaves as threats to the Jewish nature of the State. To rectify this malady they have embarked on a process of "Judaizing the Galilee" or, expropriating Arab land for Jewish settlement. Ironically, rather than defusing potential hostilities, this programme has unleashed them. On 30 March 1976, Galilee Arabs organised a strike to protest the seizure of land. The strike became a riot in which the Israeli police shot and killed rampaging Arabs. Remembered now as "Land Day", the protest has become a rallying point for the Arabs of Israel.

The continuation of land expropriation, the sense of relative deprivation experienced by Israeli Arabs as they commute between Jewish Israel and Arab Israel, the omnipotence of an antagonistic ideology and the initial Israeli response to the nascent Israeli Arab political awakening, conspire in a grim prognosis for the future of internal cohesion in the State of Israel.

Sue Halpern

BIBLIOGRAPHY

Landau, J., *The Arabs in Israel*, OUP, 1965
Jiryis, S., *The Arabs in Israel*, Monthly Review Press, 1976
Eisenstadt, S.N., *Israeli Society*, Basic Books, 1977

15 The Jewish Minority in Argentina

The number of Jews who now live in Argentina is estimated at between 300,000 and 320,000. They are not officially defined as a minority and the only legal limitation that they share with other non-Roman Catholics is the fact that the President and the Vice-President of the Republic must be Catholics. But, despite this almost complete legal equality, Argentinian Jews are seen by the majority of the Argentinian population, as they usually see themselves — as a well differentiated minority group. This differentiation is not so much related to religious considerations as to social and political ones.

Leaving aside the Marrano (crypto-Jewish) immigration of the Spanish colonial period, Jews began to arrive in Argentina in small numbers during the second half of the last century. Massive immigration started only after the wave of Russian pogroms in 1881. That immigration was organised as a scheme to involve Jews in rural and agricultural work, and at the same time, as an escape from the strong anti-Semitism prevailing in Eastern and Central Europe. The size of agrarian Jewish colonies grew gradually to a peak population of more than 30,000, but later declined in the face of economic, cultural and social difficulties. The majority of the sons of Jews went to the towns to work as artisans, merchants and industrial workers and in the next generation, many became students and members of the professions. A similar process occurred with later waves of Jewish migrants coming from Poland, Central Europe, North Africa and the Balkan Peninsula, who settled in towns. The present Jewish community in Argentina, is mainly urban, centered in Buenos Aires, with an Ashkenazi (Western) majority but with an important Sephardic (Oriental) minority of between 60,000 to 70,000 persons.

The initial aim of settling the persecuted Russian Jews in a land free of anti-Semitism was utopian. In fact, the Jewish immigrants found that although Argentina was more benevolent to them than Eastern Europe, it was still a country charged with anti-Jewish feelings. At first there was the traditional Hispano-Catholic Judeophobia, then came the waves of modern anti-semitism from Europe, which culminated in the massive impact of Nazi ideology. Consequently, Argentinian Jews were the target of chronic political aggression from conservative and clerical elements and from ultra-rightist organisations. Sometimes this aggression exploded in violent eruptions such as the *Semana Tragica* (tragic week) of January 1919, when the bloody repression of a worker's strike was accompanied by a veritable pogrom, involving attacks on Jewish areas with many people wounded and some killed.

Further, the seizure of power by the armed forces in coups in

1930, 1943, 1962, and 1976, were almost always accompanied by an increase in the political power of clerical or clerical-fascist ideologies. For Jews this meant new pressures and discrimination — most frequently murder and harassment of individual Jews, virulent anti-Semitic propaganda and the virtual closure to Jews of many military ranks and the diplomatic services etc. From 1943–45, there were also some attempts to impose legal restrictions on Jews at the provincial level, for example, the prohibition on speaking Yiddish in public places, and wholesale dismissal of Jewish teachers in the province of Entre-Rios.

The present military government does not have an official anti-semitic policy, but several government personalities (some close to the centre of power) hold strong fascist and anti-Semitic views. Jews continue to be barred from the official positions mentioned, are excluded from participation in upper governmental levels, and there are few Jewish professors at the universities, despite the numbers of senior Jewish professors and academics between 1956 and 1966. In addition to all this, there is persistent neo-Nazi propaganda which continues to reappear, despite official prohibitions by the government which evidently lacks the power or desire to end these.

The attitudes of Jews varied from one period to the next. The first generation born in the agricultural colonies, adopted an enthusiastic integrationist philosophy. They tried to integrate themselves into many sections of Argentina's economic and social life, especially in the socialist and liberal parties and cooperatives and trade unions which they had helped to create. At the same time, other sections of the Jewish population founded many Jewish communal institutions, based mainly on the models of Central Europe: synagogues, mutual aid institutions, libraries, religious and secular schools, daily newspapers in Yiddish, journals in Yiddish, Hebrew and Spanish (the latter when Jews began to abandon the Yiddish and Ladino of their parents) and Jewish clubs with tens of thousands of members.

Anti-Semitic outbursts instigated a withdrawal by Jews into their communities and institutions. A strong Zionist movement grew up with youth branches that were especially important in the Israeli period of Independence in 1948. In turn, this was followed by the passage of many Jewish youth to leftist, ultra-leftist and populist tendencies, in the general Argentinian political arena. The majority of Jewish students were involved in nonviolent (and violent) protest movements in the sixties and seventies. As a result, some hundreds of young Jews were killed, and many others disappeared, during the suppression of the guerilla organisations and other sympathetic groups, and also in the uncertain atmosphere and arbitrary violence prevailing in the last few years.

As a result, many Jews have emigrated to Israel, Spain, Venezuela, Mexico and other countries. The number of these emigrants is not exactly known but it is estimated that in the last five years, between 20,000 and 30,000 Jews have left Argentina — about one tenth of the Jewish community.

It can be said that there are three possible options for a minority: assimilation, conservation of the group's identity in situ or emigration. All three occurred among the Jewish minority in Argentina. Marriage between Jews and non-Jews is frequent — from 30 to 40% in the Buenos Aires district. The children of these marriages predominantly tend towards integration with the Catholic majority, but they are often confronted with widespread anti-Semitic prejudices and are faced with the social bars described above. The second, conservation of the group's identity, is being developed with growing intensity, partly because of the closure of other outlets for Jewish youth, but mainly because Jewish communal life has become restive and uncertain due to the physical and political attacks on it. The emigration movement may be divided into two trends. The first, to Israel, is motivated by Zionist ideology. The second, motivated mainly by personal considerations, is to other countries and includes a significant number of political refugees. Emigration is still possible from Argentina, but some European and American countries, for instance Venezuela, Mexico and Spain, place various restrictions on Argentinian immigration in general, and indirectly limit Jewish options.

The present atmosphere of political repression and anti-Semitic outbursts have compounded the already uncertain situation of Argentinian Jews. The future of the Jewish minority in Argentina remains questionable. Argentinian national ideology like that of most Latin American countries, is not based on the recognition of the existence of a pluralist society and culture.

Jose A. Itzigsohn

16 The Jews of North Africa

There are today approximately 18,000 Jews in Morocco, 6,000 Jews in Tunisia and only a handful of Jewish families in Algeria. This is in contrast to the situation 20–25 years ago. At that time there were about 275,000 Moroccan Jews, 175,000 Algerian Jews and 100,000 Tunisian Jews. Since Jews tended to be better educated than North African Muslims and were more likely to live in urban centers and play professional roles, their significance as national minorities was even more considerable than numbers alone show.   Large Jewish migrations to North Africa took place after the Romans destroyed the second Temple in Jerusalem in 71 C.E. This was almost 600 years before Islam and the Arabs entered the Maghreb. Later migrations followed the Spanish Inquisition (1490s) and Spanish Jews rarely settled in the countryside. In the cities, however, they contributed to a reorganisation and enrichment of communal life. Literacy increased, for example, and a class of prosperous and internationally-connected Jews subsequently emerged.

French colonial rule was established in Algeria in 1830, in Tunisia in 1881 and in Morocco in 1912. The French conferred many privileges on North African Jewry, partly to justify themselves as liberators and partly to divide the indigenous population. In 1870, almost all Algerian Jews were given French citizenship. Also, the Paris-based Alliance Israelite Universelle (AIU) began its work about this time, educating Jews in the language and culture of France. Jewish communities prospered under colonialism and a measure of unity emerged among Jews in each Maghreb country. There were networks of schools, clinics and religious courts, for example, newspapers and later radio programmes designed principally for Jews.

Jewish departures from the Maghreb started in 1948, when religious Jews from the Moroccan and Tunisian interior began to leave for Israel. A more important stimulus to migration was the growing cultural and political distance between Jews and Muslims. Few Jews identified with North African nationalism, and government policies promoting Arabism and Islam after independence reinforced their alienation. Since Jews were rarely literate in Arabic, they naturally feared Arabisation schemes. In addition, Jews were relegated to a permanently inferior position by constitutional provisions making Islam the official religion, while many Muslims considered Jews tainted by their association with colonialism. Thus, almost all Algerian Jews left after the Revolution in 1962 and departures from Tunisia and Morocco have been occurring since both countries became independent in 1956.

The Jewish communities remaining in Tunisia and Morocco are small and vulnerable. Their position reflects not only continuing emigration but also internal migration, a disproportionately large inactive population and the decay of communal institutions. In Tunisia, Tunis has about 4,000 Jews and is the only major centre of Jewish life, while roughly 1,100 more live on Djerba, an island that was relatively unaffected by colonialism and the AIU. There is a large number of older people, children, and indigent individuals. In Tunis, there are probably fewer than 500 families with a steady income, but the active population still spans a broad socio-economic spectrum: there are many merchants, some wealthy businessmen and professionals, and a substantial number of white collar workers.

A Central Committee in Tunis is the most important institution of the Jewish community. The Committee was once an elected policy-making body, chosen by Jews to defend their interests; today it it limited to administration activities. The Committee operates several nursing homes, a day care centre, a religious primary school, a welfare programme and a cemetary. It also has links with a large clinic and several synagogues. Schools no longer contribute significantly to the community's institutional structure. All AIU schools closed by the mid-1960s, and today many Jews attend either French schools or the school of an overseas Jewish organisation. Religious courts were disallowed after independence and so have also disappeared. The Chief Rabbi of Tunis, formerly head of the rabbinical court system, continues to represent the Jewish community and direct it in matters of ritual.

In its broad outlines, the situation of Jews in Morocco is similar although the absolute number is much greater. The community number only 6–7% of its former total, and Jews are concentrated in the largest cities, most notably Casablanca. Over 2,000 Jews live in Rabat, four other cities — Fez, Marrakesh, Meknes and Tangiers — have about 1,000 each, and several more towns have a few hundred. This population is also reasonably heterogeneous. There are numerous indigent and elderly, but many Jews are in their 30s and 40s and a substantial number are active and wealthy. Although the "institutional" capacity of the community has diminished, the Central Committee of Casablanca has more resources and facilities than that of Tunis, and committees also exist in other Moroccan cities. The same is true of education. Each year witnesses the closure of additional Jewish schools, but the AIU's Ittihad Maroc has primary and secondary schools in several cities, and there are three other Jewish school systems, as well as autonomous community schools in some towns. Religious courts also continue to function, while a National Council in Rabat oversees the central committees and assists Jews in communities without these organisations.

Although discrimination is officially prohibited, and Jews in the aggregate remain more prosperous than Muslims, Jews in both Tunisia and Morocco are relatively powerless. Each community is virtually a non-participant in national political processes and neither has any formal representation of its interests at higher levels of government. Even in Morocco, Jewish institutions operate outside rather than inside the regular structure of government. Under these circumstances, Jews must rely on personal contacts with Muslim officials to articulate political demands and they must limit their political activity to seeking redress on narrow administrative matters. Survey data shows that individual Jews are low in political efficacy and participant citizenship. Thus North Africa's Jewish minorities are dependent and vulnerable. The protection of their rights is unreliable and depends heavily on the goodwill of the majority.

The future portends continuing emigration and communal dislocation for North African Jewry; and, in addition to the cultural and political distance between Jews and Muslims, other factors contribute increasingly to these trends. Educational advances have reduced dependence on Jews and foreigners, and created pressures for economic discrimination in favour of Mus-

lims. Acts of harassment are another consideration; though officially discouraged, they occur frequently on popular levels,
especially among illiterate Muslims who are bitter about social
injustice and receptive to ideologies attributing their problem to
Zionism and colonialism. Since, too, the existence of the numbers
necessary to carry out normal social religious activities is increasingly in doubt, the attraction of emigration is reinforced and
accelerates withdrawal. In sum, the position of North African
Jewry is highly unstable. The Tunisian Jewish community is
already reaching a point of non-viability and the community in
Morocco will increasingly resemble it in the years ahead.

Mark Tessler

BIBLIOGRAPHY

Attal, Robert, *Les Juifs d'Afrique du Nord: Bibliographie*, Leiden,
1973
Chouraqui, Andre, *The Jews of North Africa: Between East and
West*, Philadelphia, 1968
Flammond, Pierre, *Diaspora en terre d'Islam*, Casablanca, 1960
Hirschberg, H.Z., *A History of the Jews of North Africa*, Leiden,
1974
Serag, Paul, *La Hara de Tunis*, Paris, 1959
Tessler, Mark, "The Identity of Religious Minorities in Non-
secular States: Jews in Tunisia and Morocco and Arabs in
Israel" in *Comparative Studies in Society and History*, 20 July
1978
Tessler, Mark, "Minorities in Retreat: The Jews of the Magh-
reb" in R.D. McLauren (ed) *The Political Role of Minorities in
the Middle East*, New York, 1979

17 The Jurassians and European Cultural Compromise

In 1951, a clause was added to the Constitution of the Swiss canton of Berne to the effect that the canton includes "the people of the original canton and the people of the Jura" (*Volk* in the German version, *peuple* in the French). It was in 1815, as a result of the Congress of Vienna, that the Jura was joined to Berne. For nine centuries it had been an autonomous Prince Bishopric of the Holy Roman Empire, for three months in 1792, an independent revolutionary republic and then, between 1792 and 1815, part of France. Had the Jura become a Swiss canton in its own right in 1815, there would have been no problem in the 1970s. To Metternich and his allies, however, it was safer to have the new French frontier manned by the strongest of the existing cantons. Thus German-speaking Protestant Berne rather gracelessly accepted a French-speaking minority with a strong Roman Catholic element and a much more radical political outlook. Yet only a few years previously, Vaud, a disaffected French-speaking territory long subordinate to Berne, had at last been recognised as a separate canton. Today, Berne an exceptionally large canton in terms both of area and population, has a million inhabitants. The seven districts of the Jura constitute a distinct geographical area to the north, mountainous, wooded and riven by gorges.

Throughout the nineteenth century, the feeling that the Jura had been cheated of its proper status found expression in a succession of autonomy movements. The degree of decentralisation and direct democracy within the canton helped to preserve French as the main language of local administration and education: even the district prefects who supervise Bernese communes on behalf of the cantonal government are elected by the people of the district concerned. In the Jura, there have been comparatively few open breaches of the unwritten Swiss "territorial principle", according to which immigrants are expected to adapt themselves to the traditional language of any commune. It was, nevertheless, a linguistic matter which, in 1947 marked the beginning of a new, sustained and militant movement to restore the ancient political identity of the Jura. In that year, the cantonal parliament declined to confirm the appointment of a Jurassian as Minister of Public Works because he could speak no German. The fierce reaction to this incident eventually led to the constitutional amendment already mentioned, and to another amendment confirming that the official language of the Jura was French; simultaneous translation was introduced into the cantonal parliament in 1954. In the meantime, the Rassemblement Jurassien, a non-party movement founded in 1948 with one aim, to make the Jura a separate canton of Switzerland, had been steadily gaining strength. During the sixties a series of tactless acts by Bernese agencies helped the Rassemblement to develop into a mass movement, while much publicity was accorded to the demonstrations of the Groupe Belier, a youth movement founded in 1962, which occupied public buildings and interrupted the Federal Parliament and international sporting events. For a time there was even a Front de Liberation Jurassienne committing acts of arson and some disaffection in local units of the Swiss citizen army. In 1965, the 150th anniversary of the joining of the Jura to Berne became, in many parts of the Jura, an occasion for joyous protest rather than celebration.

It is the tragedy of the Jura that the militancy of the Rassemblement has been matched, in word and deed, by unionist movements based on the three southern districts. These districts, closely linked with the city of Biel/Bienne (28% French-speaking and officially bilingual) are traditionally Protestant and therefore more easily assimilated into the party system of the old canton. Immigration of German-speakers into these districts was at once a source of anxiety for those who cherish the old culture and a source of loyalty to the old canton. In spite of the tendency of some Jurassiens to glorify France and denigrate Switzerland, there was no question of Jura leaving Switzerland; yet it was "separatists" and "patriots" who waged battle in the Jura, many far from being exclusively Jurassien in descent.

On the face of it the grievances of the Jurassiens were far from spectacular: their language flourishes in and out of public life; their religious grievances, real enough in the nineteenth century, belong to the past; their economic grievances, such as depopulation (the Jura contained one fifth of the cantonal population in 1900 but only one seventh in 1970), isolation from the main road network, and failure to take advantage of a strong industrial potential, acquire much of their significance from the exceptionally high standards prevalent both in Switzerland and in the adjoining area of France. What was really at stake was the identity and the self-respect of the Jura. Each predominantly French-speaking canton has a cantonal capital and government to unify it, promote its collective interests and project a distinct personality: already, in drawing up a particularly liberal constitution for their new canton, the Jurassiens gave further evidence of their markedly distinct political identity, across religious boundaries.

The French linguistic minorities in three other Swiss cantons, Fribourg, Valais and Grisons, have been integral communities of those cantons for centuries. The Bernese Government's claim that it spent more per head on the Jura than on most other regions of the canton, was beside the point: what the Jurassiens claimed was power to transform their economy so that it needed no subsidy. In Switzerland, the sense of local historic identity is particularly strong; to a significant extent, cantons are still small states in power as well as status. This helps to explain the astonishing militancy both of the Rassemblement and of their opponents.

In 1968, the Federal Government appointed a Commission to find a solution. In its first report, the Commission accepted the creation of a new canton as reasonable and worthy. Nevertheless it was felt that the local unionists had a case, and that the situation was so complex and so emotionally charged, that one referendum in the Jura as a whole could not lead to a settlement. It recommended therefore that 20% of the elctorate of any district should be entitled to demand a second referendum to decide the future of that district, followed by a third referendum to give border communes a choice. This did give the separatists an opportunity to set up a new canton without a majority in the Jura as a whole — but they had no desire to split their homeland. By this time the Bernese Government (which in 1963 still regarded the creation of a new canton as "unthinkable") had come to accept that the people of the Jura should be allowed to settle the matter for themselves: a constitutional amendment granting self-determination to the Jura was carried overwhelmingly in the canton as a whole in 1970. In 1971, the second report of the Petitpierre Commission made compromise proposals for Jurassien autonomy within Berne — while the Bernese Government too was working on alternatives to separation. But the polarisation of opinion had proceeded too far for compromise. In the referendum of June 1974, the separatists gained a small majority in the Jura as a whole (54.2% of the votes in a 91.8% poll in the six French-speaking districts; even including the German speaking Laufental the overall vote for a new canton was 51.9%). Then in March 1975, the three southern districts opted out of the new canton, though over a third of the electors voted for staying in, and in September that year, a third referendum was held in those border communes where the requisite number of electors had demanded a further poll. As a result, eight southern communes decided to join the new canton and one northern commune opted out. The Laufental (now a detached district) will remain in Berne for the time being, but may eventually join one of the neighbouring German-speaking cantons.

It is to the credit of the Bernese that they should eventually have decided, against the grain, that the Jura problem was a matter for the Jura alone. But the separatists' complaint that, only when they seemed to have a chance of winning a majority was the question of splitting the Jura first posed, has some truth. More important still, in referenda on the very unity of the Jura, the votes of unassimilated newcomers from the old canton and other German-speaking areas were often decisive — the Jura is not the only comparatively under-developed mountainous area which has to export its ablest young people and become a dormitory and a place of retirement and recreation for the cities of the plain. Who qualified for a vote was, in fact, one of the main issues considered by the Petitpierre Commission. Under Swiss constitutional law there was everything to be said for, and under international law little to be said against, accepting the principle that law should be made by those to whom it will apply. The fact remains that almost half the citizens of the southern districts of the Jura originated in German-speaking areas: the separatists maintain that there is a striking correlation between the "No" vote in each commune and the number of citizens of recent German-Swiss origin. In many closely contested communes like the town of Moutier, there can be little doubt that newcomers tipped the balance.

The admission of the new canton of Jura with a population of some 67,000 and an area of 837.4 square kilometres into the Swiss federation in a federal referendum held in September 1978, was a foregone conclusion. The constitution of the new canton had already been ratified by the electorate of the Jura and, with the exception of one clause, that of the Federal Assembly. This clause provided for the possibility of the southern districts eventually joining the Jura, subject to their separation from Berne being accomplished in accordance with law. The clause is probably repugnant to the Federal Constitution, which guarantees the territory of each canton, but it is unlikely that we have heard the last of it.

Perhaps the splitting of the Jura was the only compromise possible between a society with roots and a mobile society, between a territorial principle based on history and a majority principle based on arithmetic. But many Jurassiens will always feel that, after nine centuries, their unique homeland was split in two as a result of immigration on a scale too great for assimilation, coupled with emigration caused by a lack of positive government; that altering the character of an area by means of immigration does not cease to be imperialism when it results from blind economic forces; that withholding voting rights from recent national immigrants for a certain period is far from racialist, when the only object is to preserve the identity of a region and the variety of the world.

Outside Switzerland, it is doubtful whether a solution of any sort for the Jura problem could have been worked out so soon after the emergence of the Rassemblement as a serious force. It is indeed astonishing that, in a European climate of amalgamation and standardisation, the separatists should have succeeded in creating a new canton at all. But even in Switzerland, one can neither avoid paying a price for past injustice nor, after a lapse of time, pay that price in full without causing further of offence. The Jurassiens now have a canton of their own. They will leave behind them in Berne a deeply split French-speaking minority of 32,000 only 4.8% of the population of that canton.

Ioan Bowen Rees

18   Koreans on the Island of Sakhalin

If Captain Yossarian was the victim of Joseph Heller's "Catch-22", then 45,000 Koreans detained on the island of Sakhalin are the victims of an international "Catch-22". The Koreans were installed on the island of Sakhalin, off the coast of Siberia, in 1943 when Japanese authorities enacted the National Mobilization Act. Japan had annexed Korea in 1910 and now drafted these Koreans forcibly to replace Japanese workers who had been conscripted into military service. The Koreans were compelled to work in mines, engineering and other military facilities. They suffered from chronic food shortages and hardships; the temperature often dropped down to −22 C in winter.

On 15 August 1945, Japan surrendered to the Allied Forces but on 9 August Soviet armed forces had begun advancing on southern Sakhalin which they occupied along with the Kurile Islands by 23 August. On 19 December 1946, the "U.S.A./U.S.S.R. Agreement for Repatriation from U.S.S.R. Controlled Territory" was concluded, and the Japanese authorities took back about half a million Japanese citizens. But those who had been forcibly brought from Korea were told they were no longer Japanese citizens and were abandoned. As the repatriation ship left the coast of Maoka in Sakhalin, they sat on the ground and cried to be taken too.

Those who remain on the island of Sakhalin today are the last refugees of World War II and all are now in their 50's, 60's, and 70's. Over the years, under some pressure, the Koreans were given the choice of becoming Soviet citizens or citizens of the Democratic Peoples Republic of Korea — North Korea. Knowing that they could not go back to Japan (which refused repatriation of non-citizens) or to South Korea, which is not recognized by the Soviet Union, 65% of the refugees have selected citizenship with North Korea, 25% have selected Soviet citizenship, and 10%

have chosen to remain "stateless" because they have not given up hope of returning to the Republic of Korea (South Korea). These stateless persons suffer from many disadvantages. They cannot travel or communicate freely and they are under restrictions in regard to occupation, education, and residence. They persist, but until recently their cause was unknown to the outside world.

In late 1956, as a result of a Japanese-Soviet Communique, approximately 2,200 Koreans who had married Japanese were allowed to return to Japan. In 1958, this group of returnees organised the "Association for the Promotion of Koreans' Repatriation from Sakhalin". A similar association was organised in Korea by families of the refugees. Under continuing pressure from these organisations the Japanese government admitted moral and political responsibility for the refugees, but no legal responsibility. In these circumstances, four of the refugees, represented by 17 Japanese attorneys, sued the Japanese government in Tokyo District Court in December 1975, demanding that the Japanese government assume the responsibility, not only morally and politically, but also legally for bringing back the Sakhalin Koreans. They are also hoping to ensure procedures within international law to enable the Koreans to leave Sakhalin, through the pressure of world opinion.

Eugene Wexler

19   The Ladins of the Dolomites

Ladin, a dialect with Romansch and Friulan of the Rhaeto-Romance family of languages, is spoken in three of the northern provinces of Italy: Bolzano, Trento and Belluno. The total number of Ladins is not known, but is estimated to be about 35,000, of whom 23,500 live in these provinces. The Ladins of Bolzano (South Tyrol) numbered 15,456, 3.7% of the Province's population, in 1971; they live principally in the Valle Gardena and the Valle Badia. Those of Trento and Belluno are to be found mostly in the seven parishes of the Valle Moena and in the parishes of Cortina d'Ampezzo, Pieve-di-Livinallongo and Colle-Santa-Lucia.

The Ladins who live in these high valleys have never had any doubt about their political allegiance. Since the Venetian Wars of the fifteenth century, when they repulsed the Italians and then the French, they have usually made common cause with the largest minority of northern Italy, the German-speakers of the South Tyrol. In 1810 they appealed to the King of Bavaria to prevent their annexation by Italy and throughout the nineteenth century they fought against Napoleon's armies in defence of their traditions and liberties. Again in 1848 they resisted Mazzini by force of arms and all attempts to assimilate them under the Risorgimento failed.

Although the language was not written until 1700 and is still divided into seven dialects, it was Ladin and the work of their poets which gave the Ladins a sense of communal identity in the eighteenth century, especially by the knowledge that Ladin was a member of the Rhaeto-Romance group and was thus related to the more illustrious Romansch of the Grisons in Switzerland. But it was the rise of Italian nationalism in the nineteenth century which fostered the Ladins' political consciousness, the conviction that as an ethnic group they were strongly attached to Austria and, more particularly, to the South Tyrolean way of life which they shared with their German-speaking neighbours. Shortly before the collapse of Austria in October 1918, the South Tyrol having been invaded by Italy three years before, the parishioners of Gröden, Enneberg, Buchenstein and Fassa made their famous appeal to the German-speakers, ending "We are not Italians and have never wanted to be numbered among them. Nor do we wish to become Italians in the future. The fate of the German Tyroleans must be our fate too, their future ours. With them we and our fathers have always lived in the closest union and harmony. May it always remain so!"

In the following year the same parishes made a similar appeal to President Wilson at the Treaty of Versailles, but to no avail. With their German-speaking neighbours, the Ladins of the Dolomites were obliged to become citizens of Italy.

Up to World War I Ladin had been taught in the elementary schools but under the Fascist regime, beginning in 1921, Mussolini's policies of political and linguistic coercion were imple-

mented in all sections of public life. In this the Duce relied to
some extent on the work of philologists such as Ettore Tolomei
(1865–1952) and Carlo Battisti, who provided the Fascists with
pseudo-scientific theories which were used to claim that Ladin
was not related to the Rhaeto-Romance family but was a dialect
of Italian, and that the Ladins were therefore Italians. When it
became clear that the Ladins rejected these theories the use of
the word Ladin was promptly banned. In 1939, under the terms
of the agreement on evacuation between the Governments of
Italy and Germany, about 2,000 Ladins left the South Tyrol for
Austria in order to escape from deportation to other parts of
Italy.

After the Second World War the Statute of Autonomy (Article
87), which was passed for the region of Trentino — Alto Adige
in 1948, allowed the teaching of Ladin during the first year at
primary level. But in Trento and Belluno no such provision was
made and in those two provinces the language remains untaught
today. There have been several attempts to improve the status
of Ladins during the last fifteen years. In 1967 a delegation led
by Alois Pupp, the Ladin representative on the Regional Council
of Bolzano at that time, called for the creation of an electoral
district for the Ladin-speaking districts, equal status for German
and Ladin, and more teaching through the medium of Ladin in
the primary schools. Rome's refusal to grant these concessions
was widely criticised in the Ladin-speaking valleys. The campaign has been led since then by Guido Jori, editor of the news
bulletin *Postiglione delle Dolomiti*.

The Ladins have also formed their own movement, the *Union
di Ladins*, among whose successes was the introduction of a
weekly programme and twelve minutes a day in Ladin broadcast
by the regional radio station. This society, which publishes a bi-
monthly journal, *Nos Ladins*, has joined a students' organisation
known as *Union Generala de la Dolomites* in leading what
appears to be a revival of interest in Ladin culture. Politically,
they support the *Südtiroler Volkspartei*. One of their most serious
handicaps is that Ladin-speakers are scattered in the three
provinces and show little inclination to unite. In 1972 five of the
seven Ladin parishes in the Fassatal, increasingly disappointed
by the Regional Council of Trento, voted in favour of joining the
South Tyrol. Their ambition was thwarted not only by the local
authorities   but   by   the   Ladins   of   the   South   Tyrol

who saw in such an extension of their territory the danger of further dilution of their number by the Italian-speaking majority of Trento. A similar proposal by the *Movimento Ladini* for the reunion of all the Ladins in the Dolomite Alps within a single administrative unit is likely to remain theoretical. Not only do the Ladins of the South Tyrol — the only group of Ladin-speakers with even minimal linguistic rights — find it unacceptable, but the regional experiment in Italy, already in grave difficulty, seems incapable at the present time of such development.

Meic Stephens

BIBLIOGRAPHY

Alton, J.B., *I Ladin dla Val Badia*, Brixen, 1968
Battisti, C., *Storia della Questione Ladina*, Firenze, 1937
Demont, G., *Die Ladiner in Tirol und Friaul*, Chur, 1919
Devoto, G. & Giacomelli, G., *I Dialetti delle Regioni d'Italia*, Sansoni, 1974
Rocia, G.I., *I Ladini delle Dolomiti*, Canazei, 1966
Rocia, G.I., *Protesta del Populo Ladino delle Dolomiti*, Canazei, 1972
Salvioni, C., *Italia e Ladinia*, Milano, 1918
Salvi, Sergio, *Le Lingue Tagliate*, Milano, 1975

20 Lebanon: Composite Nation and Battleground

Lebanon was not long ago a moderate, prosperous and democratic country. Its balanced constitution held together divergent and competitive communities. Today the country has been torn apart, cities have been reduced to rubble, thousands have been killed

and many mutilated and tortured. The reasons for this breakdown
are complex and sometimes invidiously subtle.

The most obvious external factor in the breakdown has been
caused by the Palestinian refugees in Lebanon. After King
Hussein expelled the Palestinians from Jordon the refugee population swelled to 400,000, primarily Muslims, and changed the
religious balance in a country of 2.5 million people. In the secret
Cairo Agreement of 1969, which was incorporated into the
Damascus Pact of 1976, Lebanon was to give up her sovereignty
over the refugee camps and certain towns in the south: a decision
made with the knowledge that the majority of Muslims in the
Lebanese army would not fight their own people. In addition to
the Palestinian conflict on Lebanese soil, all Arab nations, the
United States, Russia, and Israel have all used Lebanon as a
battleground in their struggle for power in the Middle East.
Syria has claimed that the civil war was an Israeli-American-
Egyptian plan to draw attention away from the Sinai agreement,
while Egypt has claimed it was an American-Syrian-Jordanian
plan for Hussein to gain control over the Palestinians without
creating a separate state. Israel may also have an interest in
wanting Lebanon to fail, to prove that diverse religions cannot
live together in peace; frequent Israeli raids on south Lebanese
towns, where there were no Palestinians, have contributed to
Lebanon's downfall. Meanwhile, even if Syria cannot obtain
control of the Arab world, she has never relinquished her claim
to Lebanon as part of Greater Syria and has never recognised
Lebanon's sovereignty by establishing diplomatic relations.

The internal factors causing the breakdown are inherent in
the fact that Lebanon, rather than consisting of a homogeneous
community or having a single minority, is a composite of minorities. The major groups are *Christians*, including Maronites,
Greek Orthodox, Greek Catholics (Melkites) and Gregorian
(Orthodox) Armenians, the *Muslims* including Sunni and Shi'i,
and the *Druze*. There are also small groups of *Jews* and
Protestants.

The Maronites constitute about two thirds of Lebanese Christians. They have their own Patriarch resident in Lebanon, and
their own liturgy, but have retained a connection with Rome.
Generally they are the more successful farmers, living in the
mountain valleys, and traders. They are the most militant Christians and identify with Lebanon and the West rather than the

Arab world. The *Greek Orthodox* are closely linked with Greek Orthodox Christians of Syria through the Patriarch in Damascus; however, there are also ties with the Patriarch of Moscow who has sent several delegations to Beirut. The Greek Orthodox live mostly in Beirut, Tripoli and the southern region of Marjayoun. Because of the connections with Syria they have generally maintained good relations with Muslim rulers, but in the recent civil war they have divided their support between the Maronites and the Muslims.

The *Greek Catholic Christians (Melkites)* recognise the supremacy of the Pope, and are therefore closer to the West than their Orthodox fellow Christians. The second largest group in the Christian community, they reside mainly in Sidon and Tyre in the South and the province of Shouf in the central high plateau. The *Gregorian (Orthodox) Armenians* are distinguished from other Lebanese by their language and ethnic culture. However, they are well integrated into Lebanese society and have tried to remain neutral in the civil war.

The *Sunni Muslims* regard themselves as members of the world-wide community of Sunni Muslims and only secondly as Lebanese. Close links of kinship with Sunni families in Syria has identified them with the Arab cause. The Sunni live primarily in Beirut, Tripoli and Sidon. The *Shi'i Muslims* are the poorest, and because of a high birth rate, probably the largest group in Lebanon. There is no love lost, traditionally, between Sunni and Shi'i and as the latter live in the South near the Israeli border, they are doubly vulnerable.

The *Druze* are sometimes categorised as Muslims, but consider themselves separate. Their religion is post-Islamic and secret. For many centuries they have lived in the mountains with the Maronites and generally aligned with them politically. Approximately 6,000 *Jews* live in Lebanon and have apparently not maintained contact with Israel, but during riots the Jewish section of Beirut was heavily guarded to prevent any additional problems. The remaining population, approximately 2%, consists of *Syrian Orthodox, Syrian Catholics, Nestorians* and *Chaldaens, Latin Catholics* and *Protestants*. These groups do not have any particular political leverage.

Lebanon's solution to its plural society is unique; only Mauritius has attempted a similar plan. Instead of developing an alternative national secular identity, the Constitution, Pacts and

Statutes have all tried to balance the diverse sectarian communities. The Constitution of Lebanon seeks to safeguard its multicommunity character in specific terms: "the State shall respect all religions and creeds" (Art. 9); "Sects shall be equitably represented in public employment and in the composition of the Ministry" (Art. 95); as well as in general terms, "all are equal before the law" (Art. 7). The Constitution goes further by ordering that the State must not merely be passive but must work affirmatively to meet the expectations of the different groups.

The unwritten National Pact of 1943 had perhaps more effect than the Constitution until the signing of the Damascus Pact of 1976. In the National Pact of 1943 the Christian and Muslim leaders reached an understanding: 1. Lebanon was to be reaffirmed as an independent sovereign State. The Christians would not seek foreign protection nor would the Muslims attempt to form a political union with Syria or any other Arab nation. 2. It would become a member of the Arab family, yet not cut off its cultural ties with European civilisation. 3. Public offices would be distributed among the confessional groups including as President, a Maronite; Prime Minister, a Sunni, and Speaker of Parliament, a Shi'i Muslim.

The respect for pluralism is carried further into the Statutes and the courts. The Criminal Code curtails complete freedom of expression by threat of punishment of "any act . . . designed to ferment or having the effect of fermenting . . . disrespect for other sects" (Sec. 317). Each religious group has its own separate personal law courts and is given internal autonomy in matters of personal law such as marriage, divorce, adoption and inheritance. The State makes no provision for civil marriage or divorce.

The primary advantages of this system are twofold: while each minority group is respected, disadvantaged groups are given an opportunity for representation. The problems of this system, and the part its intricacy and delicacy have played in the breakdown of Lebanon, are not so obvious.

One of the major problems has been weak leadership. Observers have felt that this is a result of basing governmental positions on religion rather than on competence; the inept or corrupt have held power while the more able have been denied the opportunity. In the past the less educated Muslim community was more ready to accept a plan which guaranteed them representation in high political office. However, an intellectual elite emerged which felt that the National Pact had served its evolutionary purpose, and that the New Lebanese National Covenant of 1976, commonly called the Damascus Pact, should be followed. This abolishes confessional distribution and applies the principle of competence to Civil Service offices, excepting only appointments of "First Category".

A second problem has been the close identification of political parties with parochial loyalties so that they often hinder the larger national interest. Lebanon has been divided because its citizens have often regarded themselves as Arabs or Christians first, and Lebanese second. These attitudes have been encouraged by parochial schools, and by the obligatory use of identity cards stating both name and religion. The Damascus Pact recognised this problem in the clause stating: "Public Instruction shall be enhanced . . . educational curricula should be developed to pro-mote national unity." Early in 1979 all identity cards were changed to omit mention of religion.

Another problem is that this democratic constitution has been tested in a society that still contains feudal elements. In Lebanon the divisions are not merely between religions, but are also between clans. Power is often hunted through almost gangland methods.

Westerners usually often cite the need for a current census as a fourth problem. Although it is obvious that demographic patterns have changed since the 1932 census, it is not clear that an updated census would solve any problems. The relationship of the Shi'i and the Sunni is such that a change in the consti-tutional balance of power which would result under the new census would merely create different problems.

The future of Lebanon is not certain; to outsiders it appears that all that is left are belts of control. To those residing in Lebanon in many ways life is the same: there is water, electricity, telephones. Whatever the future the "scars of violence and awfulness" are there and will take a long time to heal.

Gracia Berg

BIBLIOGRAPHY

Abid, Al Maragati, *Middle Eastern Constitutions and Electoral Laws*, New York, 1968

American University of Beirut, Department of Political Studies
and Public Administration, *The Lebanese Constitution*, Reference
Edition in English, Beirut, 1960
Bulloch, John, *Death of a Country: The Civil War in Lebanon*,
London, 1977
Owen, Roger, (Ed), *Essays on the Crisis in Lebanon*, London,
1976
Salibi, Kamal, *Crossroads to Civil War: Lebanon 1958–1976*,
London, 1976

21   The Mapuche Indians of Chile

There are about half a million Mapuche Indians living in Chile
today. Most of them, about 400,000, live on some 3,300 reservations scattered throughout the southern provinces of Cautin,
Malleco and the northern part of Valdivia and extending into
the provinces of Arauco, Bio-Bio, Osorno and Llanquihue. A
further 50,000–150,000 Mapuche live in or around the urban
centres of Santiago, Concepcion and Temuco.

The Mapuche, who were the largest group of the Araucanian
Indians, resisted Inca invasions of their territory in the 15th
century. The Spanish invasion of what is now Chile began in
1541. The Spaniards enslaved and rapidly destroyed the Picunche
Indians but were met with firm resistance by the Mapuche south
of the river Bio-Bio. A century after the conquest began, the
Spanish generally gave up trying to subjugate the Mapuche and
during the following two hundred years Spanish-Mapuche relations consisted largely of sporadic raids and numerous peace
agreements. The Chileans' attempts at conquest were finally
successful in 1884 when the Mapuche suffered a major military
defeat.

The problems and oppression the Mapuche face have always
revolved around the theft of their land (the term "Mapuche"
means "people of the land") and, at the beginning of this century,

the Mapuche were herded together into a large number of small and confined reservations to make way for large non-Indian owned estates which soon began to expropriate the best reservation land as well. Left without enough land to support themselves, many Indians were forced into becoming tenant-farmers, share-croppers or, simply labourers for the large estates.

Today, as well as sharing the problems of poverty, unemployment and economic exploitation with the rest of the Chilean peasants (60% of Mapuche babies die within a year of birth), the Mapuche are also subject to the same forms of ethnic discrimination as other South American Indians. This discrimination and hostility cuts through the whole socio-economic, cultural, educational and religious aspects of Mapuche society. But, despite the fact that much of their life-style has been eroded and adapted as a result, the vast majority of Mapuche continue to form a distinct ethnic group, and maintain many Indian socio-cultural traits and ways of life as well as their indigenous language.

The State has continually attempted to destroy the Indians' traditional structures and so bring them firmly under its economic and political control. Whilst the reservation system was imposed on the Mapuche and although the reservations are hopelessly small, it is into the reservations that the Mapuche way of life has retreated and held out against its enemies. An examination of Chilean legislation affecting Indians shows that, apart from the law of 1972, nowhere is there a single expression of respect or support for the Mapuche's distinctive culture. On the contrary, since 1929, legislation has been aimed at splitting up the communally-held reservation lands into individual plots which could then be easily bought or stolen by the large non-Indian estates. Up to 1961 some 800 reservations were so divided and, although there were juridical procedures for dealing with the return of land which had been illegally expropriated, only 352 cases were upheld out of 1,434 cases brought to the courts and only 1,362 hs. of land out of the 3,380 hs. supposedly to be returned to Mapuche actually did revert to Indian ownership.

The Agrarian Reform Acts of 1961 and 1967 did restore some 1,434 hs. of Indian land over a period of 9 years. This reform was accelerated dramatically under the Allende government which, in two years, returned 72,000 hs. of Mapuche lands to their rightful owners. In 1972 a new law was passed — albeit somewhat emasculated by the Congress — which, for the first time in Chilean history had been drafted in collaboration with Mapuche. The most important points of this Act 17 729 was the return of land which had been illegally expropriated from the reservations, and the division of a reservation only when a majority of residents requested it.

The military coup of 1973 put a halt to the Reform Acts immediately and began returning land to the large estates. Mapuche who had been active during the Reform, including leaders of the Indian population, unions, ethnic organisations and peasant councils, soon saw a wave of brutal repression which included murder, imprisonment and torture. Thousands of Mapuche were reported killed. Some did manage to escape into exile and, over recent years, a number of committees of Mapuche in exile have been formed (particularly in Europe) to keep the Mapuche issue alive and press for their rights through public and private meetings and the publication of bulletins and articles.

On 28 March 1979, a new law was passed by the military junta which provided, once again, for the rapid division of Mapuche reservations; this time a reservation could be split up at the request of only one of its residents. This was presented as "emancipating" the Mapuche. The Indians themselves, however, see it is another — and perhaps final — attempt to destroy them: legalised ethnic destruction. After the initiatives the Mapuche were able to take under the Allende government, their only possible response now is to revert to a defensive mistrust. If there is any difference between the situation now and the course of their history, it is that the repression is now more successful — Mapuche are actively campaigning against it in international fora outside Chile. Over the last 400 years the Mapuche have survived numerous attempts to destroy them as an ethnic group. Compared with other South American Indian groups they are numerically very large and, although optimism might seem ill placed in the face of the brutality of the present Chilean regime, the Mapuche have survived other tyrannies.

                                                        Stephen Corry

BIBLIOGRAPHY

Berdischewski, Bernardo, *The Araucanian Indian in Chile*, International Working Group on Indigenous Affairs, 1978

Berglund, Staffan, *National Integration of Mapuche: Ethnical Minorities in Chile*, Almqvist and Wiksell International, Stockholm, 1977
Boletin Informativo Mapuche (also published as *Mapuche Voice*), nos 1–6, Indigenous Minorities Research Centre, Bristol
The Mapuche, IWGIA, 1979

22 Migrant Workers in the Gulf States

The oil price rises of 1974 have long since confirmed the Arabian peninsula — with a total population of under 20 million — as the world's richest single land area. But the generalisation needs two important qualifications; not all the countries of the region are part of the oil boom, and in those that are the resulting wealth is graded on a scale where citizenship is the only true passport to lasting riches and social standing.

The countries exempt from the boom are the Yemen Arab Republic (North Yemen) and the neighbouring People's Democratic Republic of Yemen (South Yemen). Poor enough to be included with them is Oman, where oil revenues are small and where future oil and gas exploitation is still a matter of conjecture. One further prospective candidate for this group is Bahrain, where oil reserves are nearing depletion and where the Government is adopting a strategy of industrial diversification as a means of preserving the nation's prosperity. The other countries of the area — Saudi Arabia, Kuwait, Qatar and the United Arab Emirates — are in the enviable position of possessing a seemingly endless supply of money. Their populations are so small that, if they each abandoned their massive development plans, the citizens could live off the investment income from accumulated surpluses indefinitely. Such an existence might well be the most sensible course given the potential dangers inherent in the artificial social systems produced by oil wealth. But this path will never be taken, both because the industrialised world needs the develop-

ment market potential of the region in order to earn money
with which to buy the region's oil and gas, and because the
countries themselves are too far along their present road ever to
turn back. Instead, they must learn to solve social problems which
are as unique as the wealth which brought them about.

The problems are quite simply those of population. Saudi
Arabia, the world's biggest oil exporter, has a citizen population
of around 4 million and a foreign worker population of perhaps
3 million. Kuwait has fewer than 600,000 citizens out of a total
population of 1.2 million. In Qatar, with one of the world's
largest fields of natural gas, the total population is a mere 180,000
of whom only a third at most are Qatari citizens. In the United
Arab Emirates, dominated by the oil revenue of Abu Dhabi and
the commercial expertise of Dubai, the disproportion is just as
great — about 250,000 citizens to 600,000 non-citizens. Only
Bahrain of the Gulf Sheikhdoms can point to a clear citizenry
majority among its quarter million people. The figures tell their
own story. The citizens are the minorities and the "guest worker"
immigrants are the majorities — helot classes employed to enable
the citizen elite to live a life of pampered ease.

The immigrants divide into their own ethnic groups. At the
bottom of the social heap are the Baluchis, Pakistanis, Bengalis
and Indians employed in the menial tasks as road-sweepers and
unskilled labourers. At about the same level are also Egyptians
and Yemenis, but there is another stratum of Indians and
Pakistanis who have the education to be clerks, telephone and
telex operators, and hotel receptionists. The administration, both
of business and government, is dominated by Palestinians (a
quarter of Kuwait's population is Palestinian, many of them
resident for the last thirty years), Egyptians, Syrians and
Lebanese. At the very top, acting as advisors to rulers, are
Palestinians and Britons. Throughout the whole region, with the
exception of Bahrain and the oil-poor states, it is hard to find a
real job — as opposed to a sinecure — which is not filled by a
foreigner, whether he be a grocer, an accountant, or a taxi-driver.

In such a situation, acute nervousness among the citizens is
inevitable: will the Palestinians mount a coup in Kuwait? Will
Shi'ite workers from Iran disturb the balance of Bahrain or the
conservatism of Wahhabite Qatar? Will the Yemeni labourers
and small businessmen bring the seeds of revolution to Saudi
Arabia? The reaction by the citizens is to organise ever-vigilant

— but immigrant-manned — security forces and to turn increasingly to labour from South Korea (men without their families), imported only for the specific contract length of the project on which they work.

Undoubtedly many of the immigrants — notably the Palestinians and the Lebanese — enjoy a high standard of living, and even the poorest would not be there unless his work represented a greater opportunity than any available in his own country. But this, the standard argument put forward by the citizens, ignores the indignities suffered by someone who is counted as second-class, simply because of his race. It also ignores the glaring inequalities in life-style. Citizens in the Gulf enjoy the world's most complete welfare state. Parts of this system are available to some of the immigrants, notably free medicine and free education to government employees, but the theoretical extension of charity to the immigrants cannot hide the hovels within sight of Kuwait's luxurious Sheraton Hotel, or the teeming warren of Indians and other sub-continentals within a hundred yards of Dubai' Creek.

The classic citizenry optimism is that when the time comes — when all the development projects are finished — unwanted immigrants will simply return to their homelands and that until then, none has any interest in upsetting the economic applecart. But the optimism is based on weak premises. The immigrant Arabs often feel superior to their citizen hosts in both culture and education: the Palestinians in Kuwait bitterly resent the fact that after they have built the country, they are still liable to be expelled at a moment's notice. The sub-continentals may well be more amenable to expulsion, but they will still be needed to do jobs which no citizen would touch.

An obvious solution would be to grant citizenship to immigrants of long residence and proven loyalty, a concept being toyed with by some of Kuwait's leaders. But from another view, this answer would strike at the very root of national identity carefully fostered among a citizenry whose allegiances, until very recently, were to their tribes rather than their nations. Instead, the explosive mixture of citizens, with rights and riches, and immigrants, with no rights and few riches, is set to continue as before. The oil which brought economic independence has also brought the curse of artificial societies which will need more than alert security services if they are to survive.

John Andrews

23   Minorities of the Mezzogiorno

There are three small, vestigial groups speaking languages other than Italian in Italy's southern regions. Virtually ignored by the Italian State and in the last stages of decline, they are not recognised as ethnic minorities in any special way, either politically or culturally. The official census does not enumerate them and it is difficult to say how many people belong to these communities, which are often no more than a few villages where only the older generation still cling to the language of their forebears. The Greeks, Croats and Albanians of the Mezzogiorno are, in the words of Sergio Salvi, among those who speak *'le lingue Tagliate'*, 'the severed tongues' of Italy.

According to the Census of 1921, the last to enumerate them, there were 19,672 Italians whose mother-tongue was the Italiot dialect of *Greek*, of whom 16,033 were in Apulia and 3,639 in Calabria, in the extreme south of the peninsula. Unofficial estimates in 1930 put the total at approximately 36,000 but by today, in the absence of any reliable statistics, it is generally believed that between 10,000 and 15,000 Greek-speakers live in these areas. They are to be found in two enclaves: around Salento, especially Calimera, and to the east of Reggio. The last remnants of a population which had its origins in the Byzantine invasions of southern Italy between the sixth and tenth centuries, their cultural life has declined in modern times but they produced at least one significant poet: Vito Domenico Palumbo (1854–1918), one of the participants in the Greek Renaissance. Since 1955 cultural contacts have been renewed with Greece and two magazines have been published for the promotion of Greek culture in Italy. Among its enthusiasts is Dr Giovanni Aprile, a former mayor of Calimera. But Italiot Greek is no longer used in churches or in the schools. Italian is the only language spoken by the younger generation and all the evidence suggests that the language of this minority is almost extinct.

According to a private enquiry in 1954 there were about 4,000 speakers of *Croatian* in the Molise area, but there are no reliable statistics relating to the present situation. Descendants of refugees who escaped the Turkish invasions of the fifteenth and sixteenth centuries from what is today the Yugoslav Republic of Croatia, speak a language which is an archaic form of that spoken along the border between Croatia and Bosnia. They are to be found only in three villages: Montemitro (1,469 Slavophones out of a population of 1,669 in 1954), San Felice del Molise (831 out of 908) and Acquaviva-Collecroce (1,736 out of 1,927). The numbers of Croatian-speakers decreased sharply during the Fascist years between the two World Wars. But during the last twenty years there has been a revival of interest in Croatian culture, encouraged by the Italian branch of the International Association for the Defence of Threatened Languages and Cultures. Contact with Croatia has been renewed. In 1967 the Bishop of Zagreb and Primate of the Catholic Church in Yugoslavia celebrated mass in Croatian and was rapturously greeted by the villagers. A Croatian-Italian grammar has been distributed free to every home and lessons in Croatian given on a voluntary basis. The bilingual journal *Nas Jesik/La Nostra Lingua* serves as a newspaper. Yet most observers would agree that, confined as the Croat-speakers are to a very small and poor geographical area and enjoying none of the basic rights which linguistic groups require for survival, the language is probably doomed to imminent extinction.

The population of *Albanian* origin in Italy is estimated at 260,000 of which only about a third is believed to use Albanian as an everyday language. They live, for the most part, in about a hundred districts of the region of Calabria, Apulia, Basilicate, Molise and Sicily, districts that are generally very poor and lacking any natural centre, their inhabitants mostly shepherds and farmers. The most important towns are Bronte in Sicily and Galatina in Apulia, but here Italian has replaced Albanian as the language of the majority and of day-to-day affairs. The Albanian-speakers are the descendants of the mercenaries who helped King Alfonso of Naples to put down rebellions by the barons of Calabria in the fifteenth century. Unlike the Greek and Croatian minorities, they have produced a respectable literature. Constantino Bellucci (1796–1867) was a patriotic poet who sang of the lost homeland and his hope of returning to it, while Jeronim di Rada (1814–1903) devoted his poems to the liberation of Albania from the Osman yoke. Among other Albanian writers born in Italy were Guiseppe Schiro (1864–1927) and Salvatore Braila (1872–1961), both of whom enjoyed literary reputations in Albania. A number of Albanian-speakers have held prominent positions in Italy's political and religious life, including Luigo Giuro, a member of Garibaldi's Provisional Government, Rosalina Petrotta, a deputy in Sicily's Regional Assembly, and Giovanni Stamati, Bishop of the Albanians in southern Italy. The Albanian language is studied at the Universities of Rome and Naples and, since 1945, at the Institute of Albanian Studies at Palermo. But it is not taught in the schools and, despite its comparatively strong position in a few dozen districts, it has no official status whatsoever. Article 6 of the Italian Republic's Constitution states, 'Every national minority must be protected by special laws', but attempts to implement it have so far failed.

Meic Stephens

BIBLIOGRAPHY

Aprile, G., *Traudia*, Taranto, 1950
Camai, M., *La Parlata albanese di Greci in provincia di Avellino*, Firenze, 1971
Gelcich, A., *Colonie slave nell'Italia meriodinale*, Spalato, 1908
Kotiqui, E., *Antologia della lirica albanese*, Milano, 1958
Salvi, Sergio, *Le Lingue Tagliate*, Milano, 1975
Taibbi, R. & Caracansi, G., *Testi neogreci di Calabria*, Palermo, 1959
Pulgram, E., *The Tongues of Italy*, Cambridge, Mass., 1958

24   The Muslim Minority in Western Thrace

Western Thrace, being the north-eastern part of Greece covering the area between the rivers Nestos and Maritsa, has a largely Turkish speaking Muslim minority estimated at between 100,000 and 120,000. This minority comprises mainly ethnic Turks, in addition to some 30,000 Pomaks (a turkicised Muslim people of obscure origins mostly speaking a Bulgarian dialect with Turkish as a second language) and about 5,000 sedentary Gypsies who speak Romany and Turkish. The area, which has a total population of approximately 360,000 became officially part of Greece in 1920 when it was ceded by the Allied Powers in a treaty concluded at Sevres. The Muslim population owes its continued presence to provisions in the Treaty of Lausanne of 30 January 1923: these excluded the Greek Orthodox population of Istanbul and the Muslim population of Western Thrace from the compulsory exchange of Muslim and Greek Orthodox minorities agreed upon by this treaty and granted to both communities certain rights on a basis of reciprocity (Part I, section III, art. 45). Notably, each community was given the right to administer its own religious institutions (mosques, churches, charitable institutions and pious foundations), to have a limited degree of autonomous administration of justice and to run its own educational establishments.

The early years (1920–1923) of Greek administration in Western Thrace witnessed occasional efforts at organised opposition to Greek rule and some anti-Greek guerrilla activity by elements of the Turkish population in conjunction with Bulgarian units. After the Treaty of Lausanne, however, which definitely settled the status of Western Thrace, the new situation seems to have been accepted by the Muslim population: no movement aimed at changing this status is known to have existed since then, notwithstanding the fact that a concerted effort has been made to hellenize the area from the early days of Greek sovereignty onwards. In contravention of the Treaty of Lausanne 60,000 Greek refugees from Asia Minor who had settled there were allowed to remain, while administrative and economic pressure on the part of the Greek authorities started a gradual migration of the Muslim population into Turkey. This migration increased during World War II, due to the hardship brought on by the war, and during the following Greek Civil War, when the Muslim population suffered from continuous harassment by communist guerillas as well as by the Royalist forces. In the whole period of 1939 to 1951 about 20,000 people left the region for Turkey. Migration to Turkey continues to the present day and is the main reason that the size of the Muslim minority has remained more or less stable since 1923 notwithstanding an average yearly birthrate of 28 per 1,000. In addition, owing to settlement and natural increases, the Greek population of Western Thrace has multiplied at least six times, so that the Muslim element, from being a majority, has now become a minority.

Complaints about discrimination and the existence of a semi-official policy aimed at weakening communal institutions and at inducing the Muslim population to leave Greek territory became more in evidence in the course of the 1950s when Greco-Turkish relations deteriorated as the result of developments in Cyprus. Intimidation, threats and physical assaults occurred and at least another 20,000 Muslims left Western Thrace for Turkey during this period. Conditions became even less tolerable in the 1960s, especially after the coup d'etat of April 1967 which brought Greece its military government. This trend did not change under the new regime which assumed power at the end of 1974. In particular, after the Turkish invasion of Cyprus in that year, harassment, discrimination and administrative obstruction took place on a wider scale than ever before and seriously affected communal institutions and the well-being of the community's members.

Among the various forms of individual discrimination, the following stand out as most commonly reported by Muslims in Western Thrace: real estate is not sold to them, while they are only able to sell theirs to Christians; permission to construct new buildings or to expand those existing is withheld; they have virtually no access to loans or credit, and find great difficulty in obtaining or in renewing business licences and driving licences.

In addition, Muslims are virtually excluded from careers as government employees, while in the army (military service being obligatory) Muslims are to be found in the lowest ranks only. From 1952 onwards Muslim land-owners in particular have been victimised by expropriations of sizeable areas of land in the public interest, without receiving adequate compensation. Furthermore, the re-allocation of land in Thrace which began in 1967, has proceeded at their expense: they seldom receive land of equally good quality in return. This loss of land has seriously affected the standard of living of the population, which is mainly dependent upon agriculture and livestock-breeding.

Moreover, the institutions of the Muslim minority which are central to its existence as a community — its mosques, its educational establishments, its pious foundations (*vakuf*), and its religious leadership (*muftis* and *vakuf* administrators) — are gradually being dismantled or deprived of any significance. The very life-chances of the community are consequently threatened. Incompetent and unqualified persons, who are prepared to act contrary to the interests of the Muslim community are appointed to positions of religious leadership. The appointment of a Gypsy Muslim without any qualifications whatsoever as mufti of Didymotichon (Evros province) in 1973, and the appointment of the chairman of the council for the administration of pious foundations in Xanthi — who, as chairman of a Muslim body, openly declares that he is not a Muslim — are illustrative. The latter appointment was made in 1967, shortly after the military had assumed power in Greece. Concomitantly, elections by the community of council members were abolished in favour of direct appointment by government agencies. Unlike most other measures taken under the military regime, this forced change of democratic practice has not been reversed by the new government.

Confiscation of land and of other real estate established as pious foundations has occurred throughout Western Thrace. This has considerably affected the financial basis of community life and has caused serious problems for mosque personnel and for teachers in the community's schools, since the employees often receive part of their salary from the revenues of the pious foundations. Permission to restore existing mosques, or build new ones is refused.

In the schools, the number of Muslim teachers is gradually being reduced in favour of Greek Orthodox teachers, and teaching in Greek has been increased progressively at the expense of Turkish. Moreover, the level and the quality of teaching has gradually deteriorated in the last decade or so, owing to a demonstrable preference among the Greek educational authorities to appoint less qualified teachers in the subjects which are taught in Turkish. In particular, graduate teachers of religious subjects from establishments of higher education in the Arab world are seldom appointed, while from the 1960s onwards, Greek Muslim graduates from teacher-training colleges in Turkey have no longer been appointed to Turkish schools in Western Thrace. Certificates obtained at these colleges are no longer recognised, nor do the Greek authorities recognise any other certificate or degree in Turkey. Since 1968 only graduates from a special teacher-training college in Thessaloniki, are qualified to be teachers at the community's schools. Yet student admission to this college is restricted to Greek Muslim candidates from Greek secondary schools and from the two religious institutes of the community (at Komotini and at Echinos) where the level of instruction is generally admitted to be very low. Neither are there any Muslim teachers on the college staff. Thus it is generally felt that there is an effort to create an incompetent hellenised teachers' corps isolated from the mainstream of Turkish culture and civilisation.

Intellectual and cultural isolation is pursued intensively with respect to the Pomak minority. Since 1953 an area of 2,650 square kms, covering most of the Greek part of the Rhodope mountains where the Pomak population is concentrated, was declared a military area. Ever since, movement within this area and between the area and the outside world has been severely restricted and is subject to a permit system supervised by the military authorities. In this way, the Turkish and the Pomak Muslim communities are fairly effectively isolated from each other. Pomak isolation from present-day Turkish culture is increased since mainly Ottoman Turkish, rather than modern Turkish, is being taught in the schools in the area.

The plight of the Muslim minority in Western Thrace seems to be the result of, and partly mirrors, the vicissitudes of Greco-Turkish relationships. Developments in the Cyprus problem and the treatment of the Greek Orthodox community in Istanbul have been of notable consequence. In addition, the desire to hellenize Greek territory has been an influential force in Greek policy from the day of the establishment of an independent Greece: isolation from the mainstream of Turkish culture would seem to serve this purpose. More recently, the Turkish invasion and subsequent occupation of Cyprus may have added an additional incentive for a policy directed at the dissolution of the Muslim community by attrition: the fear of a similar situation in Western Thrace at some time in the future.

For the Muslim community the increased harassment and discrimination it has experienced from the Turkish invasion of Cyprus onwards seems to have increased the sense of Turkish Islamic cultural identity which contributes to its internal cohesion. However, political realities have not been discarded, and it is well recognised that the present state of the Greco-Turkish relations leaves little room for political initiatives or manoeuvring by the Turkish government on behalf of the Muslims of Western Thrace as has occasionally happened in the past. Lately, some of the Muslim community have made an effort to inform the outside world about its plight, publishing an enumeration of the various forms of discrimination and harassments experienced by the Muslim minority in an open letter to the Greek Prime Minister, Mr Karamanlis, and to the United Nations Commission for Human Rights. The two Muslim members from Western Thrace in the Greek Parliament have taken initiatives to give greater publicity to the community's complaints and the local Turkish press is becoming more articulate in expressing the various grievances. Lately, the authorities in a number of Arab countries, notably Egypt, Libya and Saudi Arabia, have also taken an interest. An Egyptian fact-finding delegation visited the area in September 1978. These more recent developments may be the beginning of a new era for the Muslim minority in Western Thrace, whose members claim nothing more than their rights as human beings and as citizens of the new Greek Democracy.

F. de Jong

BIBLIOGRAPHY

Andreades, K.G., *The Moslem minority in Western Thrace*, Thessaloniki, 1956

Aydinli, A., *Bati Trakya Faciasinin Icyuzu* (The Inside Story of the Tragedy of Western Thrace), Istanbul, 1977

Balic, S., "Muslims in Greece", *The Islamic Review*, xl 35–37, Woking, 1952

Bayulken, U.H., "Turkish Minorities in Greece", *Turkish Yearbook of International Relations*, iv 145–164, 1963

Dede, A., *Rumeli'nde Birakilanlar (Bati Trakya Turleri)* (The abandoned of Rumelia — The Turks of Western Thrace), Istanbul, 1975

Fragistas, C.N., "Le Droit musulman en Grece", *Annales de la Faculté de Droit d'Istanbul*, iii/4, 129–141, 1954

Zecherli, S., *'I Thraki. Apo tous archeous chronous mehri Simera* (Thrace: from antiquity to the present), Thessaloniki, 1976

25   The Pacific Islanders: An Outline

Scattered over the 64,000,000 square miles of the Pacific Ocean are groups of islands, some populated — Paradise islands of screen and dreams — others too inhospitable to bear vegetation, let alone animal or human life. After centuries of colonisation, both strategic and absent-minded, by France, Britain, Japan, the U.S. and pre-World War I Germany, groups of these islands are reaching for independence. The populations are varied, and must be the descendents of waves, eddies and drifts of migration across many thousands of miles, predominantly from the land-base of Indonesia and New Guinea. Broadly, they are divided into *Melanesians, Micronesians* and *Polynesians*.

The last occupy an enormous triangle in the Western Pacific, reaching from its apex in Hawaii, to New Zealand in the East (intersected by Fiji and several Melanesian groups) over to the South American continent. Within this area fall the French overseas territories (the Society Islands, including Tahiti, Tuamota, Austral, Gambier, the Marquesas), Samoa (U.S.) and Western Samoa, the Cook Islands (including phosphate rich

Nauru), Tonga, Pitcairn (N.Z.), and the Easter Islands (Chile) as well as Hawaii and New Zealand already mentioned. Islands within each group may be hundreds of miles apart, and inhabited or subsequently "discovered" over many different centuries. Before air transport, still accessible to the few, any sense of unity among the groups that may be conveyed by their collective names, was merely administrative convenience. Distance and sparse populations still lend a particular problem to political recognition and action, and to economic self-sufficiency.

Polynesians have the most Caucasoid features of the Pacific Islanders, with light brown skins; they are South East Asian in origin and probably migrated about 2,000 years ago. Numbers have dropped significantly over the past hundred years since records, or at least estimates, began. Once, for instance, the population of the Marquesas was 100,000; today it is 5,000: the three-sided "fatal impact" of Western contact - disease, trade and Christianity. Fatal diseases with an immediate effect on the demography include VD, smallpox, whooping-cough, measles and influenza. "Black-birding" was the name given to raids on islands all over the Pacific, but in particular from Easter Island, stealing semi-slave labour for Peruvian and Colombian mines. Christianity brought "one more thing to fight about" and a little, somewhat ethnocentric and pious, education. Today, the decrease continues, largely through migration to New Zealand and the U.S. in search of employment.

Polynesians are described as the most "Westernised" of the Pacific Islanders which also means, with the exception of some of the Marianas, that they have lost most of their culture. Hawaii is now the 50th state of the U.S., and considerable racial mis-cegenation has taken place amid the mainland Asian and white migrants and the indigenous population; yet the original Hawaii-ans are as neglected a minority in their own land as the mainland Indians. Samoa was the centre of dispute between Germany, Britain and the U.S. before World War I. Eastern Samoa was eventually taken by the U.S. and remains in constitutional limbo. Neither a union state, nor an incorporated territory or common-wealth, it has been particularly prone to unchecked twentieth century buccaneering, with some commentators using the expres-sion "ethnocide". Certainly, the fishing grounds has been seized by U.S. and Japanese interests, as a low-wage, high export fishing industry, with imported tinned tuna taking its place in

the local diet. Western Samoa was given to New Zealand as a
League of Nations Trust territory after the First World War,
and gained independence in 1962. Compared to American Samoa,
New Zealand's trusteeship was relatively protective and benign.
Samoan society was very complex, with a strong *matai* (chief-
tainship) organisation of economic distribution. The *matai* system
survives as the official political form of representation, but it is
conservative, weak and defensive, resented by the young, who see
it as betraying its main purpose. With half the population under
15 today, and with the impact of foreign fishing, banana and
other export industries, it is predictable that Samoan society will
disintegrate further. The problem remains with what is it
replaced?

The Cook Islands, whence the Maoris migrated to New
Zealand, became virtually "independent" in 1965, but the New
Zealand government retained control of foreign affairs, defence
and finance. A hospitable people, the Cook Islanders became
landless in their own land, to make way for fruit plantations.
Today "the soul of the place is slipping through many busy
fingers". Fruit remains the main export, but food must now be
imported, and the economy is necessarily subsidised by the New
Zealand government.

Melanesians is the general term applied to the inhabitants of
the South West Pacific excluding New Zealand but including
Papua New Guinea, which is the third largest island in the
world and will not be discussed here. The term covers a great
variety of human type: "some biological differences between
human beings within a single race may be as great as or greater
than the same biological differences between races" (Howells).
Inhabitants of the Pacific for over 30,000 years, it is by language
that they are linked; however, Melanesia means "islands of the
dark people", and general characteristics include small stature,
very dark skin and broad faces with rounded forehead. They are
subsistence farmers growing yam, sago, bananas and sweet
potatoes, but pig and fish form a considerable part of their diet.
Pigs are also a form of currency and form an integral part of
ceremonial activities. The Solomon Islands (formerly U.K.) are
mountainous, well-watered, forested and thickly populated
(178,940 in 1973) islands. Guadalcanal, of World War II fame,
is the largest and culturally the most diverse. Copra and timber
are the main export, and plantation labour requirements have

broken local society here to a very great extent. Wage employment is replacing subsistence agriculture, but is very vulnerable to fluctuations in the price of copra in international markets. While improved medical knowledge has lowered the child mortality rate, and countered the effects of European disease, the new diet of imported foods bring dietary deficiencies, malnutrition and secondary diseases. The Solomon Islands were granted independence in July 1979. The main difficulty facing the new government will be balanced, decentralised development. The New Hebrides constitute an 80-island shared "condominium" between France and Great Britain. It has a dual police force (not without a reputation for violence), and a strong Nationalist Party led by a French priest. The French imported Tonkinese (North Vietnamese) to work the coffee, palm and fruit plantations, and there has been some inter-racial antagonism. There are 950 overseas companies (mostly French), and 8 banks based in the capital, because the New Hebrides have been declared a tax free zone. Symbolic dance and intense ceremony still form an important part of Melanesian cultural existence, particularly in the more remote islands, but tourism is beginning to destroy what trade and mining has not.

New Caledonia, on the Tropic of Capricorn to the east of Australia, constitutes French Polynesia. While manganese is among the exports of the New Hebrides, nickel forms 96% of New Caledonian exports. French Polynesia has always been the most highly politicised region of the Pacific. Racial conflict dates back to the first French settlements, and land confiscations. The French were discouraged from using local slave labour in the nickel mines, and instead brought in convicts, and later indentured Asian labourers (Chinese, Japanese, Vietnamese). The indigenous population dropped substantially. In the twentieth century, it has been the use of the area for atomic testing that has stimulated political activity. General de Gaulle high-handedly dissolved all local political parties in 1963, and several leaders (often of mixed blood) have been imprisoned since. There is a non-governmental programme to render the area a nuclear-free zone, but the French government has suppressed such opposition to its nuclear activities. Overseas French citizens are able to vote and send representatives to the Paris Assembly, but an autonomy movement is growing, arguing that the French government has violated Article 74 of the French Constitution and Article 77 of the U.N. Charter. A small commando group has started taking violent action.

Straddling Melanesian and Micronesian culture are the Gilbert and Ellice Islands, which were until recently administered jointly by the U.K. The former belong firmly geographically within Micronesia — a terminological combination of Greek "mikro", little, and the Asiatic "nesia" meaning islands. The other groups within the area, which lies to the north of the equator, are the Marianas (northernmost) including Guam, the Carolines in the west and the Marshall Islands to the east; all are U.S. administered. They are largely "high" islands, tall volcanic outcrops, but some low coral atolls amid them are inhabited — habitable land is scarce. Micronesians also display greatly different physical characteristics, and there are 11 mutually unintelligible languages. The Marianas were first "discovered", not without bloodshed, by Spanish explorers. The Japanese took over from the Germans after World War I, and developed intensive sugar plantations. Used as naval bases by the Japanese in World War II, they were later to become the sites from which the Hiroshima bomb was flown. Guam in particular became the base from which B-54s attempted to destroy Vietnam. The Marianas were a U.S.-administered post-war (strategic) Trust Territory and were only formally acquired as the "Commonwealth of the Northern Marianas" in 1977. There is little evidence that the U.S. improved the life for the inhabitants during its trusteeship, neither developing the economy on their behalf, nor restoring idylls. Indeed the change of status brought a form of local government, but for only 14,000 recognised citizens (excepting Guam) and was intended to sanction the building of further air and naval bases — with US$10,000 per head being paid into the local economy. Between U.S.$50 and 100 million worth of fish have been taken from the area by foreign companies, while $80 million has been allocated to build a base in Tinian. Employment of local labour is low, companies preferring to import Filipino and South Korean labour. In Guam, where the air-base population is over 100,000 there are only 4,800 legal aliens, and as many illegal. There have been admitted abuses by the Immigration and Nationality Service in the import of foreign labour. Peonage has been known in the seventies, and now a minimum wage has been established. A Chamarro newspaper exists, but this smothered society has very little chance of genuine political or cultural self-determination.

The Marshall Islands are a double chain of coral islands, with a small (24,000 in 1972) fairly homogenous population, but they include the Bikini and Enewatak islands where the first 23 Atom bombs explosions took place. Some defiant return settlement by displaced islanders has taken place in islands within 100 miles of Bikini, although not declared nuclear-free, and an independence movement is gaining strength. Micronesian society is very concerned with status and prestige, enhanced by a rich mythology of ghosts, spirits and deities. Land is the principal font of political power and spiritual life and consequently the loss of territory has a dual significance, in both economic and cultural deprivation.

Ocean Island and Nauru, both phosphate bearing were managed and mined by the British, with Australia collaborating in Nauru. The latter declared its own independence in 1968, but Ocean Island has been the centre of an intense legal battle with the British government. Prevented from declaring independence from the Gilbert Islands, by whom it is administered, compensation for loss of land and personal inconvenience has been minimal for Ocean Island's Banaban people, now removed to Fiji, while phosphate extraction has brought them no income and only profitted the British companies concerned.

This outline can only convey a few aspects of the irreversible impact of Western life on remote societies, first in its insatiable, competitive, acquisitive nineteenth century form; latterly in its insatiable, competitive, acquisitive twentieth century form. Replacing Christianity, "modernisation" is the new religion. Many Europeans genuinely believe they are improving "primitive" life with the one or the other, but unless constitutional machinery can be developed to redress economic abuses, the "improvements" are rendered almost as destructive as the callous neglect in international Trust or the cynical abuse of political responsibility. The remoteness of these varied islands brings into stark relief the conflict of centre and periphery in underdevelopment, more often described in other contexts. Yet this very remoteness could also isolate the "treatment" for the ills of too rapid and too uneven post colonial economic "development". Without exception, the Pacific Islands would benefit from some reordering of the international economic order. As new and largely weak governments, born of very different colonial administrative traditions, with vast distances separating their citizens, they have difficulty staking a claim to true economic independence let alone enforcing it. As more and more island groups achieve political independence, they join the United Nations as the one forum in which they hope to be able to express their long suffocated and confused aspirations, and to seek recognition for their very existence.

GA/RF

BIBLIOGRAPHY

Binder, Pearl, *Treasure Islands: the Trials of the Ocean Islanders*, Blond and Briggs, 1978
Brookfield, Harold (ed), *The Pacific in Transition: Geographic Perspectives on Adaption and Change*, Edward Arnold, London, 1973
Gale, Roger, *Micronesia: Lynchpin of America's Future in the Pacific*, Pacific News Service, San Francisco, 1972
Howe, K.R., *The Loyalty Islands: A History of Culture Contacts 1840 to 1900*, University Press, Hawaii, 1978
Howells, William, *The Pacific Islanders*, Weidenfeld, Nicholson, London, 1973
Moorehead, Alan, *The Fatal Impact*, Hamish Hamilton, London, 1966
Todd, Ian, *Island Realm*, Angus and Robertson, Sydney, 1973

26   Papua-New Guinea: A Nation of Minorities

Papua New Guinea, one of the most recent Third World countries to gain its independence, presents a fascinating example of the problems created by the confrontation between the rights of minority groups within a state and the policies of a national government seeking to promote the interests of the state as a whole or, at least, the interests of the most powerful political grouping in the state. While Papua New Guinea resembles many other Third World states in certain areas it is clearly distinguishable by its massive tribal and linguistic fragmentation which has had an important bearing on the overall outcome of the contest between the central government in Port Moresby and the hundreds of minority groups which make up the state. Central to the nature of this outcome has been the struggle over the creation of a constitution and body of civil laws which minorities in Papua New Guinea look to for the protection of their rights and interests. The passing of the Constitution into law on independence in September 1975 by no means saw the end of this debate, but rather marked an unsatisfactory attempt to force a resolution in the face of an impending political and economic crisis. Since then a series of Organic Laws, standing mid-way between the Constitution and civil laws enacted by Parliament, have gradually helped to form an outcome more acceptable to both minority groups and the national government.

The state of Papua New Guinea is comprised of the eastern half of the island of New Guinea, which lies just to the north of Australia, and a number of smaller islands extending northeast to Bougainville Island at the northern end of the Solomon Archipelago. The diversity of the country's traditional society is somewhat overwhelming. Amongst the 10,000 or so tribes over 700 distinct language groups have been identified and even where two neighbouring tribes shared the same language there was no guarantee that mutual hostility, and the resulting isolation, would be any less. Instead, as Charles Rowley has noted, the small inter-village trade that did exist in some areas did little to break down a village's traditional isolation, in which it remained ". . . cut-off from others by barriers of suspicion, by warfare and especially by fear of sorcery." As a result the profusion of social and cultural characteristics equalled that of languages and in an attempt to produce a general classification of New Guinean society Rowley finally suggested that the term "Melanesian" could be used, as long as it was taken to refer more to a common predicament rather than any clearly distinguishable social system.

In the light of these observations it could be assumed that there are considerable difficulties to be met in examining the role of minorities in a country where the traditional social and cultural order has been comprised of nothing but minorities. However, the arrival of Europeans and the changes brought about during the period of their administration fundamentally altered the traditional status quo in two equally important aspects. The first of these was the establishment of a Western political structure based on clearly defined territorial boundaries and the right of a central administration to govern within these boundaries. Although there are important differences in the way in which the Australian Administration and, after 1975, the National Government gained the right to govern within the country they both proclaimed that their policies were designed to further the "national interest." This is quite simply the course of action that can be said to benefit the majority of individuals living in the state. In other words a hypothetical dominant group with no linguistic, cultural or political ties comes into existence and it is against this "majority" that minorities (which are bound and identified by linguistic, cultural and political ties) must strive to protect their interests. In a sense this is the paradox that is to be found in examining a "nation of minorities" and it is one which the Australian Administration (somewhat belatedly) and the government of Michael Somare have sought to reduce through their efforts to foster a national identity.

The second important change brought about by over seventy-five years of European and Australian administration was less intentional, though also unavoidable as major, if not radical, changes occurred in the social and political environment. In the space of one lifetime the majority of Papua New Guinea's two and a half million inhabitants were swept from an isolated existence in stone age hamlets into a world where communication via radios, aeroplanes and trucks radically altered their perception of themselves and others. At the same time it also became possible for villagers to vote in national elections and to enrol their children in a school system which culminated in a national university in Port Moresby. Under these circumstances new identities started to form and increasingly tended to replace traditional bonds built on tribal and village identities as determinants of an individuals political orientation. This transition is certainly not uniform across the country or total where it has started to occur. It has, however, played an important part in the formation of new political groups within the state which have sought to protect minority interests.

These new identities have primarily developed around the

administrative patterns imposed on the country by the various European and Australian administrations. The most important of these patterns proved to be the division of the entire country into districts, which functioned as the principal sub-national administrative unit throughout the Australian period of control. As a focus for popular identification the district gained its potency from the fact that its organisation and operation were of considerable significance for the day to day lives of villagers. Its acceptability as the basis for a new group identity was further strengthened by an expatriate habit of stereo-typing Papua New Guineans according to the district from which they came, and the tendency for villagers themselves to identify with their home district whenever moving outside it, particularly to seek employment or education.

Although most districts were themselves fragmented by tribal and linguistic divisions this does not appear to have greatly hindered the development of district political identities. Two factors in particular seem to have been influential in this respect. The first of these is that the problems which faced one particular village within a district tended to be common to all other villages in the district, regardless of language or tribal affiliation. If, for example, the district was allocated too few resources, or was isolated by sea or a mountain range from the decision making centre in Port Moresby, then the villagers of the district suffered as a whole. At the same time many tribal and linguistic groups were too small to effectively protect their interests and while various attempts were made to promote sub-district local government councils (often combining as many as thirty villages) these met with little success as they did not correspond with any comparable administrative unit with significant decision making authority.

Therefore, by the late 1940's, when most of the country had been brought under the control of the Australian Administration, the thousands of separate village groups which made up the traditional political fabric of the country found themselves in a position where the possibility of their interests being sacrificed in order to achieve Administrative ends was very real. Individually there was little they could do; however, by the late sixties a combination of events in certain areas of the country hastened their amalgamation into larger political units which could more effectively promote and protect their interests. That this event tended to take place outside Administration attempts to foster political development through the establishment of multi-village Local Government Councils is not surprising, as these enlarged minorities saw their main opponent to be the Administration. By the eve of independence in 1975 this process had spread to most districts in the country and the demand that these new district based political identities be recognised was being expressed not only in submissions to the Constitutional Planning Commission, but also by the threat of secession in the case of Bougainville District.

While the Australian Administration avoided seeking an accommodation with these new political forces, through fear of encouraging fragmentation which might retard the country's economic development and endanger its political unity, this was not a course which an independent Papua New Guinean government could follow. Before turning to examine the solution put forward by the national government it is worthwhile briefly tracing the emergence of these new political identities, particularly in the district of Bougainville, which is comprised of Bougainville Island and some smaller, surrounding islands and is separated from the New Guinea mainland by some four hundred miles of ocean.

Minorities Under the Australian Administration

Australia's involvement in Papua New Guinea was, from the beginning, primarily dictated by her own defence considerations. The Japanese occupation of Papua New Guinea during the Second World War only provided further confirmation for the need for Australia to create a friendly and stable neighbouring state to the north which would act as a buffer against political disturbances in Asia. To achieve this end it was important that a unified and economically strong state be created and, in line with this, priority was given to rapid economic development as well as education and political development programmes which fostered national unity. Such programmes readily accorded with Australia's publicly stated concern to bring Papua New Guinea to independence with a sound economy and a stable, democratic government. Although Australia initially set no time limit on this task, continual pressure from the United Nations induced a marked increase in pace from the early sixties. Accordingly the

Administration became less willing to tolerate impediments to either the rapid economic development of the country or the promotion of national unity.

However, in two areas the Administration found itself opposed during the late sixties by well organised, indigenous political movements which sought to protect the rights of local people and to oppose Administration policies judged to be hostile to their own interests. On the Gazelle Peninsula, in the New Britain district, the Mataungan Association, led by Oscar Tammur and John Kaputin, gained almost total support amongst the Tolai people in opposing the Administration's attempts to introduce economic and political changes which were regarded by the Tolais as a threat to their traditions and their right to organise their own affairs. For the purposes of this paper, however, the conflict between the Administration and the Bougainvilleans is of more interest for it represents the first coalescence of a district wide political identity. Undoubtedly this process was helped by Bougainville's physical isolation from Port Moresby, the fact that Bougainvillean's very dark skin pigmentation makes it relatively easy to distinguish them from other Papua New Guineans, and the presence of large copper deposits at Panguna, in central Bougainville, which were to prove vital to Papua New Guinea's future economic development.

Though Bougainvilleans initially lacked the unity of the Tolai people (nineteen different language groups have in fact been identified in the Bougainville District) the growing discontent among the different tribal groups with the changes being brought by European planters and a mining company, combined with an apparent lack of concern for their welfare in the Administration, gradually created strong, new bonds of fellow feeling. While a history of growing dissatisfaction and dissent can be traced back to the islanders' first contact with Europeans at the start of the century, the advent of a large scale copper mine at Panguna in central Bougainville provided the focus around which Bougain-villeans could unit in their opposition to the Administration. The course of the conflict was marked by disputes over particular issues, such as land ownership and the payment of royalties. However, behind these disputes lay a growing distrust of the Administration and outsiders in general, which was matched by a corresponding desire amongst Bougainvilleans to have greater control over events which immediately affected their lives.

To the Australian Government, the Bougainville Copper Project represented a major step forward in strengthening the economy
of Papua New Guinea and reducing its dependence on Australian
aid grants. The desire that the project proceed quickly and
unopposed is reflected in the following statement by the Administration's Treasurer, Mr. Newman:

> However, the project promises such far reaching benefits for
> the Territory that the Administration must press on to bring
> it to fruition ... The Administration has a threefold financial
> interest in securing the early achievement of export production
> — as a taxing authority, as a potential shareholder, and for
> balance of payments reasons. ...
>   ... The Administration (therefore) has the responsibility to
> ensure that the various mining and land leases are granted
> without delay.
>   (Statement made in the House of Assembly, 16 June 1969)

By the time this statement was made, the Administration had
already acted positively on a number of occasions to ensure the
success of the venture. Not the least of these was the signing of
the 1967 Bougainville Copper Agreement with Conzinc Riotinto
Australia, which committed the Administration to providing the
necessary land (an estimated 50,000 acres would be needed) and
infrastructure for the project (including a port, roads, communications, a power plant and a town). As part of the Agreement
the Administration was given the right to take up a 20% equity
in Bougainville Copper Limited (BCL, the joint company formed
to run the project). Bougainvilleans, it should be noted, stood to
gain no direct benefits from this agreement as royalties from the
sale of copper concentrate would go directly to the Administration.
    This, in fact, became the first major bone of contention between
Bougainville and the Administration and was seized on by Paul
Lapun, then the member for Bougainville Open, who demanded
that 5% of all royalties be paid to the villagers on whose land the
copper had been discovered. Although the Administration was
able to block this demand the first time it was put forward in the
House in 1966, Lapun repeated the demand in 1967 and this
time was successful. While Lapun undoubtedly had considerable
support amongst Bougainvilleans in this dispute the following
conflict over the Administration's compulsory acquisition of land

required for mine and port facilities provided an opportunity for villagers to demonstrate their growing unity. Here the Administration resorted to flying in police to evict villagers from the disputed land and in an effort to organise their resistance Bougainvilleans founded *Napidakoe Navitu* ("Napidakoe" represents a contraction of the names of three local language groups while "Navitu" means "association"). Fourteen months after its initial meeting in July 1969 it had gained over 6,000 members from 116 villages in the Kieta sub-district and, in so doing, had achieved a degree of unity amongst the local clans and language groups that no other organisation, including the Kieta Local Government Council, had been able to.

Although Napidakoe Navitu made no direct gains in pushing its case before the Administration its meeting with the Australian Prime Minister, John Gorton, and representatives of Bougainville Copper Limited were more productive. Following these negotiations BCL reduced its land requirements and offered the landowners considerably better terms, from which they stood to gain approximately A$300,000 — a figure which contrasted sharply with the Administration's initial offer of A$30,000 under compulsory purchase.

In the following months leading up to the 1972 general elections two significant developments occurred which worked to further strengthen the unity of Bougainvilleans. In Port Moresby, students and trainees from the Bougainville district held a number of meetings between 1968 and 1972 to which leading politicians and civil servants from the district were invited. At these meetings the district's grievances were discussed and proposals for unified action were put forward, including the possibility of secession as a last resort. This development was mirrored on a larger scale in the Combined (Local Government) Councils Conferences in the Bougainville district which, though powerless as a decision making forum, did provide an opportunity for the numerous differences which still divided Bougainvilleans to be clarified and, in part, resolved.

Self-Government and the Constitutional Debate

In the 1972 elections Michael Somare's Pangu Party came to power in a coalition government with the support of politicians from most districts in Papua New Guinea, including Bougainville. Three of Bougainville's four MHAs were given important tasks in the country's first national government: the portfolio of mines to Paul Lapun, Business Development to Donatus Mola, while Father John Momis was made Chairman of Committees, Deputy Speaker and, later, Deputy Chairman of the Constitutional Planning Committee. For several months after this election it appeared as if the country had at last achieved political unity and stability. This impression was further enhanced when Somare released his government's Eight Point Development Programme which stressed rural development, decentralisation, localisation of control over economic development, self-reliance and the equal distribution of development spending. Although implementation of these principles would require several years of gradual re-adjustment, they did represent a marked change from the underlying philosophy of the previous Five Year Plan formulated by the Australian Administration. This plan had stressed export-led growth with major incentives to foreign investors and few restrictions on their operations. While this programme would have eventually enabled Papua New Guinea to dispense with Australian aid, required to balance the national budget, it also encouraged uneven economic development as government financial and administrative resources were concentrated in those areas which would provide the quickest and most substantial increases in production, particularly for export.

A more significant step taken by Somare's government was the appointment of the Constitutional Planning Committee to draw up a constitution for an independent Papua New Guinea. One of the major questions to be considered by the Committee was the political structure of the new state, with particular reference to the problem of whether significant powers should be decentralised from the national to the district level. In the following months the CPC toured throughout Papua New Guinea meeting villagers, representatives of local government councils and various other local groups. In both its interim and final reports the CPC stated that it had found almost unanimous support for a decentralisation of power to the district level and backed up its own recommendations in this area with supporting reports prepared by overseas constitutional specialists who also recommended a devolution of decision making power and administration. This, the CPC argued, would not only allow villagers to feel they had some real control over local affairs and to identify with the process of government, but would also provide a framework within which groups such as the Bougainvilleans could feel that their rights and interests were sufficiently protected to encourage them to remain within the state. The CPC went on to recommend that the term "province" be substituted for that of "district" and that the legislating and taxing rights of provincial governments be safeguarded from interference by the national government by inclusion in the country's constitution (from which they could only be removed by a three-quarters vote in the National Parliament).

While Somare's government expressed its approval, in principle, of the CPC's early recommendations, its attention was more closely focused on developments in the Bougainville dispute which, in the long run, represented the crucial tests of decentralisation policies. Secessionist feelings were suddenly revived on Bougainville by the news of the pay-back murder of two Bougainvillean civil servants in the New Guinea highlands on Christmas eve 1972. A general distrust of other Papua New Guineans had already been developing in Bougainville as a result of the occasional drunken and violent behaviour of labourers brought in from other districts to work on the copper project. The murder of the two Bougainville civil servants only reaffirmed the growing belief amongst Bougainvilleans that Papua New Guineans from the mainland represented a direct physical threat to their wellbeing. In the following months the Bougainville Special Political Committee (BSPC) was established to draw up a submission for the CPC concerning the urgent need for provincial government in Bougainville and to press the national government to agree to these demands. Somare's government was, at first, unwilling to accede to the BSPC's demands, but after protracted negotiations it was agreed that Bougainville was to be allowed to proceed with preparations for provincial government, provided the legislative framework developed for this move could eventually be applied to all districts. Rapid progress was made in this task, and in mid-1974 the national government passed a bill allowing for the establishment of an interim provincial government in Bougainville.

Despite the agreements already reached, the funding of the Bougainville provincial government was to provide difficult and protracted negotiations which nearly collapsed into violence on both sides. It was eventually decided that after 30th June 1975 all royalties from the copper project would go straight to the provincial government, while further funds would be provided through the annual negotiation of Bougainville's capital works programme with the national government. It was in negotiating the grant for Bougainville's first annual works programme in 1975 that the rupture which the national government hoped to avoid did eventually occur. While a simple misunderstanding of each others case prompted this breakdown, its development into a major rift was the result of the mistrust and hostility that had developed in Bougainville during the protracted negotiations leading up to the establishment of the interim provincial government.

For the national government this breakdown of understanding with Bougainville was a clear signal that proposals for the devolution of power were unworkable, at least in their present form. There was also considerable concern in Somare's government that although the principal of decentralisation to the district level was acceptable, the actual division of powers between the two levels of government as envisaged by the CPC was less acceptable. Without agreement on this crucial point, and faced with a crisis on Bougainville only weeks before the granting of independence, Somare took radical action. On the 30th July 1975, Somare suddenly broke into the debate on the final sections of the country's constitution to move that the provisions for provincial government be completely removed from the constitution. As the correspondent for the *Far Eastern Economic Review* noted, "... there was little debate and the motion was passed in 20 minutes by 40 votes to 19, the remaining members being absent from the parliament." One month later, and only two weeks before the granting of national independence, Bougainville's leaders unilaterally declared their own independence from Papua New Guinea and established the independent Republic of the North Solomons.

The Organic Law on Provincial Government

Although the independent government established on Bougainville after secession was able to gather some funds through taxes imposed on various local companies, the issue of royalties from the copper project was still unresolved. In January 1976, Bougainville gave the national government in Port Moresby five days in which to hand over all royalties. The national government ignored this ultimatum and, as a result, violence broke out in Bougainville and considerable damage was done to property belonging to the national government. Within the national parliament this action provoked numerous calls for the army to be brought in to suppress the revolt on Bougainville. Somare, however, resisted these demands and instead sought further talks with Bougainville's leaders based on revitalised proposals for provincial government. In line with this move Somare appointed Oscar Tammur, a leading proponent of decentralisation, as full-time Minister for Provincial Affairs, while also making further concessions, particularly on the question of royalties.

Bougainville's leaders in turn withdrew their more radical demands and, after several meetings with national government ministers, signed an agreement on the 7th August 1976 (the North Solomons Agreement) which marked their return to membership of the now independent state of Papua New Guinea. Within the Agreement the representatives of both Bougainville and Port Moresby recognised the principle of decentralisation at the national, provincial and local levels. Agreement was also reached on a number of other points, including the maintenance of a single public service and the need for provincial governments to have exclusive rights to legislative and taxing powers in certain areas.

The specific details for the devolution of powers were now, however, to be embodied in an organic law, rather than the Constitution (in which only the principle of decentralisation to provincial government remained). The failure to reach agreement on the actual division of powers between the two levels of government had been a major factor in the collapse of proposals for provincial government immediately prior to independence. The same problems were now met again, and in late 1976 Somare presented the necessity for overcoming these problems to the National Executive Council in the following terms:

> ... If approval of the division of functions is delayed, the repercussions will be wide and severe. The North Solomons Agreement committed us to a tight timetable. If we falter now, the North Solomons, and other Provinces, could claim — with reason — that we had failed to abide by our promises and policies. The implications of that include fragmentation of the

nation and turmoil on the eve of elections. At the least, there could be an impossible situation for Ministers to face with the electorate. At the worst, we could expect secession — perhaps more than one breakaway.

This time agreement was reached, and in early December the government fully outlined its proposals for the division of powers in the national parliament. Two months later the Organic Law on Provincial Government, in which both the legislative and taxing powers of provincial governments were embodied, was passed by parliament at its second reading. In Bougainville there was a corresponding drive to fulfil the requirements stipulated under the Organic Law for the granting of provincial government. By November 1977, these requirements had been fulfilled and Bougainville was granted full provincial government. Where Bougainville had led, other districts now rapidly followed. Considerable preparations had already been made in several other districts for the establishment of provincial government even before independence. During 1977 and 1978 the Eastern Highlands, East New Britain and New Ireland were also granted full provincial government status.

One of the few remaining problems to be met in the implementation of provincial government was opposition within the civil service, where it was feared that decentralisation of administration represented a direct threat to the power of central departments and to the career prospects of individual civil servants. The international consulting firm, McKinsey and Company Incorporated, was called in to identify the areas within the civil service where opposition was strongest and to recommend a corresponding course of action which would both assure civil servants of their future and enable the decentralisation of specific administrative functions to be effectively carried out. The government accepted the report presented by McKinsey and set out to implement its recommendations in three stages during 1978. Considerable success was met in this project, which removed the last remaining barrier to the establishment of effective provincial governments throughout Papua New Guinea.

The Future

There seems little doubt that Bougainville would not have returned to the fold without significant concessions on the part of the national government in 1976. These concessions amounted to an official recognition of the fact that a strong sub-national political identity existed in Bougainville and unless some political accommodation was reached with it, then the unity of the state would be seriously endangered. For the Bougainvilleans, the Organic Law on Provincial Government embodied most of the concessions they sought from the national government which would enable them to control the day-to-day government which more immediately affected their community. Although these concessions were not as securely entrenched as they might have been had they been included in the national Constitution (as originally intended by the CPC), they did represent an important devolution of legislative and taxation powers to the district level.

This was a move which the Australian Administration had remained unwilling to make, and which was still opposed by some within the independent state as economically expensive and an encouragement to national fragmentation. However, at the same time it can be pointed out that the very maintenance of the heavily centralised political and administrative system inherited from Australia would have led to the further aggravation of hostility against Port Moresby at the district level and a corresponding heightened sense of separateness. In this respect the establishment of provincial government was a move which the national government could not afford to reject.

In this chapter one type of minority group has been considered — the geographically specific community for which the possibility of some form of sub-national government provides a viable method for the protection of their specific interests within a larger state. However, as the CPC noted in its final report, a fundamental block exists to be ready adoption of this course of action, which is that ". . . politicians at the national level are unlikely to seek to transfer their powers to subordinate levels of government." That this transfer was eventually carried out in Papua New Guinea was, to a significant extent, due to the conciliatory attitude of the national leader, Michael Somare, who publicly staked his political future on his ability to retain Bougainville within the independent state of Papua New Guinea without recourse to the uncertain outcome that would have resulted from the use of military force. Undoubtedly, one of the key factors behind Somare's adoption of this course was the realisation that whatever accommodation was reached with Bougainville would soon have to be reached with other districts. Because of this the North Solomons Agreement of 1976 was formulated within specific guidelines which would enable the establishment of similar provincial governments in other districts without endangering national unity. This process has so far proved effective in restraining secessionist movements which might otherwise have seriously damaged national unity. At the same time, it has also provided minorities in Papua New Guinea with a more effective guarantee that their interests will be protected. The economic development of Papua New Guinea might well be retarded to a degree by the establishment of provincial governments but it was a course which the national government could not politically afford to avoid.

John Martin

BIBLIOGRAPHY

Conyers, Diana, *Planning for District Development in Papua New Guinea,* Discussion Paper No 3, New Guinea Research Unit, Boroko, 1975

Conyers, Diana, *The Provincial Government Debate: Central Control versus Local Participation in Papua New Guinea.* Monograph No 2, The Institute of Applied Social and Economic Research, Boroko, 1976

Fisk, E.K., *New Guinea on the Threshold,* Australian National University Press, Canberra, 1967

Hannet, Leo, "Bougainville Independence." *New Guinea* 4, 1, April 1969

Mamak, A. and R. Bedford, *Bougainvillean Nationalism: Aspects of Unity and Discord,* Bougainville Special Publications No 1, Christchurch, 1974

May, R., "The Micronationalists: Problems of Fragmentation," *New Guinea,* 10, 1, May–June 1975

Rowley, Charles, *The New Guinea Villager: The Impact of Colonial Rule on Primitive Society and Economy,* Praeger, New York, 1966

Skeldon, Ronald, *Regional Associations in Papua New Guinea.* Discussion Paper No 4. The Institute of Applied Social and Economic Research, Boroko, February 1977

Woolford, Don, *Papua New Guinea: Initiation and Independence,* University of Queensland Press, Australia, 1976

27 The Pennsylvania Germans

King Charles II of England granted the colony which is now the state of Pennsylvania to William Penn in payment of a debt to Penn's father. In doing so, the English King rid himself of many Quakers (Penn's supporters) who proved to be bothersome in those times of religious disagreement. Penn founded Pennsylvania as a refuge for oppressed religious groups, and to the Protestant and Anabaptist peoples of the Palatinate and Switzerland, Penn's colony was the promised land. Religious wars, famine and government restrictions had uprooted and oppressed many groups, who found themselves on the wrong side of the lines drawn at Augsburg and Westphalia. Penn's colony had the most liberal constitution (charter) of the time and above all it recognised no established church. The Palatinate Calvinists, Swiss Anabaptists and dissatisfied Lutherans along with French and Walloon Huguenots and Dutch Anabaptists, who had incorporated themselves into the German community, began leaving Europe in late 1670's. Some went to Georgia, others went to the Mohawk Valley in New York, but the overwhelming majority settled in southeastern Pennsylvania and neighbouring Maryland. By the time of the American War for Independence, the Swiss and German community in Pennsylvania numbered 100,000. It is this isolated group of German-speaking people that became known as the Pennsylvania Deutsch or Pennsylvania Germans (also called Pennsylvania Dutch, as a result of an early mis-translation of the word Deutsch).

Today the Pennsylvania Germans number about one million people, dominating four Pennsylvania counties (York, Berks, Lebanon and Lancaster) and forming large minorities in ten other Pennsylvania counties and two Maryland counties. They can be divided into three basic groups: The Plain People, who include the Amish, Mennonites and the Brethren (50,000); The Church People, who are the descendants of the Reformed, Lutheran, Moravian and a few Catholic immigrants who presently retain the German dialect and a few traditions (300,000+), and finally those who are German in surname and accent, but who have lost their traditional ties with the German-speaking community due to their proximity to other cultural areas (Philadelphia and the Anthracite Coal Region are the best examples) or due to their own efforts to be more sophisticated and cosmopolitan Americans (800,000+). One out of six Pennsylvanians has some German blood, but the educational and social institutions of both the state and the nation tend to devalue the worth of the German culture. Other than the Plain People, few Pennsylvania German children are taught the dialect and old customs and crafts are rapidly disappearing.

The Plain People and some of the Church People retain the customs and aspirations of their faltering culture. The Plain People, named by their dress, wear no ornaments, buttons or collars. Their clothing is largely black, with some blue, white or magenta shirts and dresses. The men wear broad-brimmed black felt hats and grow beards after they marry. The women tie their hair in buns and wear small white "prayer caps". The Plain People have refused all modern conveniences such as indoor plumbing, electricity, automobiles, radios, televisions, etc. Many refuse to be photographed or own mirrors believing that vanity is the worst of sins. They travel in horse-drawn buggies, grow grain, tobacco, vegetables and livestock, work from dawn to dusk and live a cloistered and narrow life; yet their language lends itself well to poetry and humour, their cuisine is very popular with the hundreds of thousands of tourists who come to the area annually and many of the farmers are immensely wealthy in spite of their self-deprived modes of living. In spite of their religious sternness, the folklore of the German region is full of witchcraft, herbal medicine and demons. On their barns, they paint hex signs to keep demons away and superstitions are evident in everyday life. But the isolation and hence the continuity of the culture has been broken and with disastrous results in many cases.

Apart from the general effects of America's anti-agrarian "sophisticated" trends, the Pennsylvania Germans are victimised in many other ways. Discrimination comes in two basic forms: employment discrimination against German-accented people outside the immediate German area and legal discrimination against the Plain People.

In the labour market and the cultural scene, the Pennsylvania Germans are looked down on, largely due to the simplicity and unsophistication with which the Germans conduct their lives. The non-Germans talk in terms of "the dumb Dutch", a phrase which has always had both serious and mocking connotations. To those Germans aiming for higher socio-economic status or intellectual recognition, the attitudes of the outside world are never forgotten and many people of Pennsylvania German descent (Dwight Eisenhower and Clark Gable as two examples) never identify themselves with the German community. A few, such as writer Conrad Richter, become the champions of their culture.

Discrimination against the Plain People is much more serious. To the tourists, the Amish country of Lancaster County seems to be a peaceful, backward paradise, but hard feelings are evident once one looks past the quaint countryside. The Plain People, though fragmented into numerous sects, are opposed to the "worldly" values of modern society and for this reason they have resisted the compulsory education system in areas where there are no schools of their own. Periodically, cases arise in which parents refuse to send their children to school. One such dispute was the case of Honeydale, Chester County in the late 1950's, where eleven fathers refused to send their children to the modern school provided by the state. The result was the establishment of a makeshift school in a farmhouse. Pennsylvania law now allows the Old Order groups to leave school after eight years to work on farms, but questions as to the quality of parochial education are still unanswered.

The Old Order groups view insurance of any type as a denial of God's providence. This belief has brought the Plain People into conflict with the Federal Government concerning Social Security legislation. As pacifists, the Plain People refuse to participate in war. After a long battle during World War I, these groups along with the Quakers were listed as conscientious objectors and were allocated public service jobs during wartime. However their pacifist beliefs are only the surface of a greater philosophy. Several sects of Plain People deny the use of coersion of any type. They refuse to participate in the legal system in any capacity, as a vital aspect of their concept of "Christian love". This protest against the existing legal system causes them great difficulties and prevents them from using the courts to their advantage.

Various Pennsylvania German groups have left Pennsylvania and established colonies in Virginia, Ohio, Maryland, New York, North Carolina and further afield. Some have gone as far as Canada and South America to seek the isolation their culture requires. Wherever the Plain People have moved they encounter serious social, political and legal problems due to their beliefs. Some have returned to Pennsylvania, where conditions are usually more favourable. In many ways they can be compared with the Flemish in Belgium, before the rise of the Flemish Movement in the late 19th Century. Depending on the events of the next decade, they could either become extinct as a culture or rise to face the demands of 20th Century society and revive their language, customs and communal spirit. The Plain People, who retain their ethnicity and their primitive communist society, have fought hard for their rights, but any revival will depend on a rebirth of enthusiasm among the Church People. Several newspapers and a bit of radio programming is the sum of the German-dialect media and the impact of modern American values drives deep rifts into German-American unity of any sort.

Hence the Pennsylvania German community is struggling to survive against the very foundation of modern American society. The Plain People have rejected modernisation, materialism and economic growth, but yet they cannot isolate themselves from the effects of modern society. The Church People and Fringe People have to varying degrees adapted to the American way of life, but yet many represent an unwillingness to fit into either the role of an isolated, rural German-American or a full-fledged cosmopolitan member of the American rat race. But all three groups will someday face the test that will make or break their culture and along with it the ideals behind William Penn's promise of unmolested liberty.

Randall Fegley

BIBLIOGRAPHY

Aurand, A. Monroe, *Early Life of the Pennsylvania Germans*, Harrisburg, 1946

Salisbury, W. Seward, *Religion in American Culture*, Homewood Ill, 1964
Schreiber, William I. *Our Amish Neighbors*, Chicago, 1962
Wilson, Bryan, *Religious Sects*, London, 1970

28 The Poles of Westphalia

In the *Land* of NordRhein-Westfallen (North Rhine-West-phalia), around the towns of Essen, Bochum and Dortmund in the Ruhr areas of the Federal Republic of Germany, there is a small and scattered number of people who are of Polish descent. It is impossible to know how many, or what proportion, are still able to speak Polish, for their existence is not recognised by the census. But they are believed not to exceed 5,000.

The grandparents of these *Westfalcyks*, as they call themselves, were agricultural workers from the province of Poznan and Silesia in Poland who came between 1860 and 1914 in their hundreds and thousands to find work in the industrial areas of the Ruhr. In 1905, the General Miners' Union of Bochum recorded that over a third of its members were 'Prussians of Polish extraction', while in the Graf Schwerin Pit the figure was as high as 52%. Employed in dangerous conditions which few Germans would accept, they developed a high degree of solidarity among themselves and continued to speak Polish underground. Their influence was so widespread that there were fears that the Polish language would become predominant in some districts. But they were soon subjected to the German Government's policies of assimilation. The Royal Office of Mines responsible for the Graf Schwerin Pit refused to publish safety regulations in Polish, and the language was prohibited in all public meetings. The Poles retaliated by forming their own union, which in the following decades, up to the time of National Socialism, became a powerful force in the German miners' union movement.

At the same time the Poles developed their own societies and

clubs, based mainly of their Catholic faith and the choral music
tradition: in 1912 there were 1,038 such groups with 111,000
members, about 40% of the ethnic group. They thus created a
framework in the Ruhr within which the tradition from a rural
to an industrial way of life could be achieved. Under the Weimar
Republic many Polish organisations were banned, never to reappear. The Polish Mineworkers' Union, which in 1919 still had
46,000 members, was wound up in 1928, in the same year as the
Polish Party which had represented the minority's interests up
to then. The 250 church societies disappeared shortly afterwards.
From 1924 many Poles began using the German version of their
names and by 1939 over 240,000 had officially abandoned their
Polish patronymics.

Westphalia had been transferred to the Reich by the Treaty
of Versailles in 1919. Between the Wars the *Bund der Polen in
Deutschland* (League of Poles in Germany), founded in 1922,
had become an influential body responsible for running secondary
schools, cooperatives and banks, but in 1939 it was prohibited
by Hitler. It was not until 1945 that the League, now with its
offices in Bochum, reassumed its former role in the cultural and
political life of the area. Today its President is the priest Edmund
Forycki. No longer influential and counting a high proportion
of old people among its members, the League confines itself
mainly to religious affairs and cultural contacts with Poland. It
organises pilgrimages, publishes a magazine *Ogniwo* (Bond)
which sells about 3,500 copies monthly, and co-ordinates the
programmes of choral societies which are still active and popular.
In the mining town of Catrop-Pauxel there is a famous choir
known as *Harmonia*, once 140 strong but now only a tenth this
size. A dozen teachers are paid by the *Land* authorities to give
instruction in Polish to about 400 children in 20 schools and 9
priests care for Polish-speaking Catholics in towns of the Ruhr.
Not prepared to disclose its membership figures, the League
claims that they were strengthened during and after the Second
World War by Poles deported from Poland. Its aim is "to keep
alive the Polishness of our fathers" in Germany.

Relations with the Socialist People's Republic of Poland have
suffered since 1945 on account of the marked clerical attitudes
of the League. The principle that "Catholic Church and nation
have always been one in the Polish consciousness and must
remain so" caused a split in the membership of the League in

1950. The *Westfalcyks* must have viewed the Pope's visit to Poland in 1979 with surprise. Cultural contacts with Poland were opened in 1962, particularly by a new body called *Zgoda* (Harmony). It has been under close scrutiny from the German authorities following a newspaper report in 1972 that 6,000 young Polish-speaking Germans were being trained as partisans in military camps organised by the Polish Army. But this was no more than a rumour, easily explained by the *Zgoda's* newspaper *Glos Polski* (Polish Voice) when it announced details of its scheme for sending sixty children to holiday camps in Poland once a year. The controversy raged for six months but has now ended and the German Government is satisfied that *Zgoda* does not receive instructions or finance from Warsaw.

It is evident that most *Westfalcyks* or 'Poles of the second and third generation' (the term *Polacke* is considered perjorative) know of their Polish descent only at second-hand and are therefore close to becoming completely extinct as a recognisable ethnic group. For them, the words of their folksong *Jeszcze Polska nie zginea* (Poland is not yet lost) no longer reflect the reality of their situation.

Meic Stephens

29 Puerto Rican Americans

According to the 1970 Census there were 1,454,000 Puerto Rican Americans living in the U.S.A. (811,000 born in Puerto Rico and 636,000 born on the mainland) 60% live in New York State (especially New York City), 10% in New Jersey, the majority of the rest in the other north eastern States. Puerto Rico's population was 2.75 million in 1970.

Originally inhabited by Taino Indians, Puerto Rico was 'discovered' by Columbus, colonised by Ponce de Leon in 1508, and remained a Spanish colony until Spain ceded it to the U.S.A. as a result of the Spanish-American war in 1899. It is a Caribbean island, 1,000 miles to the south west of Florida, and west of Cuba and the Dominican Republic. The early American governors largely ignored the island people's problems until, in July 1952, the U.S. government established the Commonwealth of Puerto Rico with powers of local self-government under a U.S. appointed Governor, but without a voting representative in the American Congress. Today Puerto Ricans enjoy many of the rights of American citizens, they are allowed free movement between the island and the mainland, and they do not have to pay federal taxes unless established residents of the mainland, in which case they assume full American citizenship.

Puerto Rico has undergone considerable development in recent decades and the Americans have large investments in the island including a substantial military base, reflecting the continuing strategic importance of the island. Since the 1920s there has been an influx of Puerto Ricans into the U.S. mainland (except during the depression and the war years), and two way migration is a common phenomenon. Demand for labour on the mainland was an important factor in encouraging such movement, reflecting the high unemployment rate in Puerto Rico (today it remains twice the U.S. rate).

About half the Puerto Ricans are white, the rest being a mixture of Spanish and African slave and/or Indian descent. Many of the more negroid Puerto Ricans are keen to emphasise their Spanish heritage in order to avoid confusion with American blacks. Puerto Rican's have the lowest income of any ethnic group in New York, and many seek public welfare assistance; however, they may still earn more than they would in Puerto Rico. The islanders come to the mainland in search of better work opportunities, but often find only low level work, particularly in the service trades. This is seldom secure employment, but at the same time good English is not usually required. There are at least 4,000 small Puerto Rican businesses in New York, but these tend to be a vulnerable source of income dependent on the limited incomes of the neighbourhood and their 'ethnic' tastes.

Most Puerto Ricans in New York have relations on the island and links with their towns of origin remain strong. Some migrants represent extensions of their extended families or communities, migrating temporarily or seasonally to the mainland. Consequently in addition to those who wish to integrate but cannot, there are those who do not wish to integrate but simply to share the intermittent benefits of American society whilst remaining essentially Puerto Rican. On return to Puerto Rico they are likely to have acquired some skills and more education than those who have never left. Many who do return to the island eventually return back to the States.

There is still marked discrimination with regard to employment opportunities especially for the darker skinned male Puerto Ricans; but there are increasing job prospects as government employees under affirmative action legislation. Data on employment rates and occupational skills suggest that opportunities are increasing particularly amongst women, but not at a rate sufficient to enable them to reach equality with the majority of the population.

Those Puerto Ricans who have not succeeded in being assimilated often invest their hopes in their children, but those in the ghettos are unlikely to get sufficient education to break out. Standards are low, and there is a high drop out rate. Even so, migrants to the States tend to be better educated than the average inhabitant of Puerto Rico, for the quality of education on the island has usually been poor. Educational attainments are improving but not at a rate to ensure equality with the Anglos. Thus, many youngsters face a future at the bottom of the social ladder.

There is a relatively high rate of drug addiction amongst the young, and also many medical and mental health problems due to poor sanitation, crowded living conditions and the stress of living in an alien culture. Problems with the law are frequent especially due to the involvement of Puerto Ricans with drugs and vice. Also, frustration breeds violence and it is deemed unsafe by the Anglos to venture into the Spanish ghettos. The whiter and better educated Puerto Ricans find it much easier to integrate into American society and those that remain in Spanish speaking communities are united by a culture of poverty rather than a common Hispanic heritage, as Puerto Rican culture both on the mainland and the island is being profoundly Americanised. To the usual problems of adjustment faced by immigrants, are added a range of racial ambivalence and identity problems.

According to J.P. Fitzpatrick (Puerto Rican Family 1971) the rate of assimilation now is comparable to that of all European immigrants in the period 1908-1912, which indicates a reasonable rate of absorption. There has been a steady increase in intermarriage particularly amongst second generation mainland Puerto Ricans; one third of those living in New York State are married to whites and outside New York it is as high as two thirds. Various self-assistance agencies are growing stronger and more influential, for instance, *Aspira* (in education) Puerto Rican Forum (in community affairs), Puerto Rican Family Institute (Social Services), and the Puerto Rican Merchants Association (commerce). The office of the Commonwealth of Puerto Rico serves initially as an orientation centre for newcomers, as well as an employment agency and legal defence organisation; thus it is the official representative of the communities, and is supported by government funds, but it has been said to unwittingly stifle the impulse towards self help.

Attachment to family and "machismo" are the most typically "Latin" traits that survive amongst these people. The family is the institution which faces the most direct shock of culture change and it also provides the greatest strength for its members in the process of change. There is still a deep sense of family obligation and *compadrazgo*. The household rather than blood ties tend to be the basic social unit in New York. The traditional extended family unit is less evident amongst the more affluent. But parent/child relationships have undergone a major change; children are no longer submissive to the authority of their elders, who are upset by the more aggressive modern attitudes and behaviour of their young; parents are especially disturbed by the threat they perceive to the virtue of their young daughters (illegitimacy in New York State increased from 11% in 1957 to 20% in 1970). "Machismo" has been undermined as women tend to have more success in finding jobs than the men, thus creating greater female independence and male insecurity. Also the traditional male emphasis on personal trust of individual rather than systems and organisations has encouraged the average American view that Puerto Ricans are less efficient.

In the early 1970s there was one Puerto Rican member of Congress, two on the New York City Council, one member of the New York State Senate and two in the State General Assembly.

There is a growing but not very unified independence movement on the Island of Puerto Rico, partly in reaction to the spread of American as opposed to Hispanic culture, partly to

take the Puerto Rican economy out of large U.S. corporation
hands, and partly to stop the "bleeding" of Puerto Ricans into
the U.S. Puerto Rican-U.S. trade is heavily in favour of the U.S.,
which finds the island a convenient and relatively docile market
whose purchasing power has been slowly increasing. On the
other hand the U.S. government has been urged to incorporate
Puerto Rico fully as a member of the American Union. (This is
opposed by those mainland Americans who feel that the U.S.,
already the fifth largest Spanish speaking country, should not
make itself vulnerable to yet more Hispanic migration). A third
impulse is to retain Commonwealth status, extending autonomy
to other institutions. Culturally and politically Puerto Rico is an
island in search of an identity, ambivalent, like the Puerto Ricans
in New York, about the embrace of Uncle Sam.

P.J. Viggers

BIBLIOGRAPHY

Cooper, P. *Growing up in Puerto Rico*, Arbor House, New York,
1971
Dworkin, A.G. and Dworkin, R.J. *The Minority Report*, Praeger
Publishers Inc, New York, 1976
Fitzpatrick, J.F. *Puerto Rican Americans: The meaning of
migration to the mainland*, Prentice Hall Inc, 1971
Gerassi, J. ed. *Towards Revolution Vol 2: The Americas*, Wei-
denfield and Nicholson, 1971
Howard, J.R. *The Awakening Minorities*, Transaction books,
Aldine Publishing Company, 1970
Kramer, J.R. *The American Minority Community*, Thos. Y.
Crowell Company, 1970
Mindel, C.H. and R.W. Habenstein (eds), *Ethnic families in
America*, Elsevier Scientific Publishing Co Inc, 1976

30 Racial Balance in Kenya and Tanzania: A Comparison

Whereas race relations commentary on East Africa tends to concentrate on the treatment of Asians and Europeans after the divestment of British colonial status, this paper examines internal African group relations. The population of Kenya and Tanzania comprise affiliations of minorities, whose cultural pluralism encompasses wide social, ethnic, religious, and linguistic geographic-regional differences — sharing Swahili as a lingua franca. The existence of powerful minorities in Kenya necessitates "racial bargaining" to maintain stability. The Kikuyu, Luo, Luhya, and Kamba tribes and the Kalenjin-speaking cluster each form 10% or more of the population. The Kikuyu are the most numerous, wealthiest, best positioned, and arguably, best educated. Tanzania on the other hand is little affected by tribal rivalry in the presence of approximately 120 tribal groups, none of which is pre-eminent.

At Kenya's independence the Kikuyu had competitive advantages: social and economic mobility within their society; relative group solidarity, access to education and adaptability to Western methods; and proximity to Nairobi. Inter-tribal rivalry had been exacerbated by the Mau Mau anti-colonial insurgence of 1952–1956. Many who opposed the revolt were killed by their countrymen, more were killed by colonial forces, often composed of indigenous (mostly Kamba) "Home Guards". The forcible movement from European farms in the "White Highlands", promoted group unity among the Kikuyu, who also supplied most of the Mau Mau fighters. Many others, however, were "Loyalists" co-opted by the British; politicians and civil servants trusted by the British could move into key positions. A large proportion came from Kenyatta's Kiambu area, the most favoured group among Kikuyu. (Rival groups are the Muran'ga or Fort

Hall and Nyeri). Tensions surrounding loyalty and terrorism have lingered. After independence, the Kikuyu population grew fastest. They took over from Asian traders, bought land from other tribes, moved into "white" farms and foreign businesses and improved their strong position in government and bureaucracy. Together with the Luo, they have dominated the power structure.

Despite British efforts to foster tribal federalism in Tanzania to ease administration, ethnic communities have not coalesced to the same extent. British administration, however, which took the form of League of Nations Trusteeship, was light in comparison with the former German colonists there, and there was far less British settlement. The Chagga (about 3% of the population) were the most advanced, by European standards, at independence. They lived in the fertile Kilimanjaro area, derived cash from banana and coffee co-operatives, and had ample educational facilities afforded by Christian missionaries. Yet the Chagga have not capitalised as much on their relative head start as have the Kikuyu in Kenya. No one tribe in Tanzania possessed the combination of size, centralised power, economic advancement, or enforced unity. The economic, and formerly political, capital of Tanzania, Dar-es-Salaam, is on the coast, an area of great tribal intermixture. Nationalism is a stronger force than regionalism: the phenomenon of "retribalisation" as ethnic groups reunite after migration to urban areas is not as prevalent as in Kenya.

Ethnic identification is not always traditional: it may arise from a crisis or a modernisation process, or can be conjured by political leaders. These can also encourage tolerance, if they so choose. Both Kenya and Tanzania officially favour racial equality and harmony. President Nyerere established early a policy of non-discrimination towards non-Africans, promoting similar attitudes among African groups. He warned that African would-be exploiters should not replace privileged Europeans and Asians. A 1964 directive sought to abolish racial discrimination in civil service recruitment, training and promotion. At its founding the Tanganyika (later Tanzania) African National Union (TANU), had pledged to fight "tribalism and all isolationist tendencies amongst Africans and to build a united nationalism".

At independence, President Kenyatta promised there would be no discrimination, colour bar or racial inequality in Kenya.

Concerning tribal preference, he gave "categorical assurance" that under the Constitution all tribal land was "entrenched in tribal authority" and no other tribe could take it. Until Kenyatta died in 1978, there was a consistent but not conspicuously successful effort at power-sharing through ethnic arithmetic. Kenyatta's first efforts to blend tribally based alignments were in vain. The leaders of the Kenya African Democratic Union (KADU) disowned him as a tribal rather than national leader. KADU, prior to its eventual amalgamation with KANU, was a coalition of Rift Valley and coastal tribes, led by Ronald Ngala, whereas KANU was basically Kikuyu, Luo (under Oginga Odinga) and Kamba. In later years, leading up to Kenyatta's death (in 1978), KANU became almost dormant. There was a political fragmentation of tribes, weakening their force as a political base. The smaller clan-sized constituency had become the basis for patronage. By 1966 the focus was on "Kikuyuisation". Executive power in Kenya is invested in the President. He appoints the Vice-President and Cabinet, removable at his will. Over 20 ministers and almost 40 assistant ministers allowed for tribal distribution, but real decision-making power rested with the 6 or so in Kenyatta's "Inner Cabinet" dominated by Kikuyu, mainly from Kenyatta's Kiambu clan. The more numerous Nyeri and Muran'ga members of parliament felt excluded. J.M. Kariuki, the Nyeri leader, was only an assistant minister when, in 1975, he was murdered in circumstances suggesting official complicity. He was a vocal critic of the elite. There were parallels with the murder in 1969 of Tom Mboya. Although a Luo, he did not appeal to tribal chauvinism, but like Kariuki had a trans-tribal power base and was a likely successor to Kenyatta. Mboya's assassination united many Luo behind Odinga, strongly associated with leftist government opposition, in his Luo Kenya People's Union (KPU). Anti-Kenyatta demonstrations prior to the October 1969 election led to the banning of the KPU and again in 1974, Odinga was prevented from running as a KANU candidate. (He was later to be imprisoned). Resistance took the form of not voting for incumbent official candidates.

Even the new President, Daniel Arap Moi, a Kalenjin, then Vice-President, was threatened by an unsuccessful attempt to change the constitutional power whereby he was to be Kenyatta's immediate successor (for 90 days) as Acting President. Kenyatta did take away Moi's power over the police and para-military

General Service Unit (GSU), which were then party again to some of the conspiracies against Moi's eventual succession in 1978.

President Nyerere also has strong powers, but Tanzania does not have parallel ethnic vying for position at the executive level. More power is vested in the party than in Kenya's de facto one-party system. TANU has rejected local party selections based on tribal ties. Elections take the form of competition between two or more Party nominees in a locality. Campaigning in a language other than Swahili is forbidden, as is discussion of tribal or religious issues. Tribal associations were originally eligible to affiliate with TANU, but by 1960 were being refused. Tribal trade unions are now officially discouraged. Consequently, TANU shows no significant over-representation of any one tribe; although the non-Christian, less educated groups are perhaps under-represented among members of the National Assembly. Political involvement is encouraged, working towards the good of the whole country. The party structure permeates society outwards from the 10-family "cell", creating an alternative national focus. Progress is perceived as requiring overall co-operation. In 1977, after the assassination of the imperious Sheikh Karume, the mainland TANU united with Zanzibar's Afro-Shirazi Party as Chama cha Mapinduzi (CcM). Its constitution seeks to ensure that there is no racial discrimination and that "all public institutions give equal opportunity – irrespective of race, tribe, religion or status".

No institution in Kenya is as poweful as the central bureaucracy, but Kikuyu are disproportionately represented in all. Their share of influential positions increased between 1969 and 1972, while the Kamba, the second most favoured, declined. The army provides an example. As a colonial remnant, the army was dominated by Kamba, more trusted than Kikuyu. By 1978 the Kikuyu had achieved parity by packing enlisted ranks, increasing Sandhurst training for Kikuyu officers and promoting them more rapidly. This process was accelerated after an abortive coup in 1971 involving some Kamba officers. The GSU of some 2,500 men was almost exclusively Kikuyu — a counterforce to the army. The way to a civil service job is believed to be through nepotism. The majority of senior posts go to Kikuyu. In 1968 there was a demand that parliament investigate the senior positions and distribute them proportionately. The motion was rejected.

There is no process equivalent to "Kikuyuisation" in Tanzania. With their educational advantages and assertiveness, the Chagga benefitted as Africans replaced European civil servants, and (a 1963 inquiry reported no substance to charges of nepotism), they maintain a strong position within the civil service. This position is not reflected in TANU leadership, probably partly because the Chagga, unlike the Kikuyu in KANU, did not seek political prominence before it became obvious that TANU would triumph at independence. TANU has tried, when not inappropriate, to post party functionaries some distance from their tribal homelands to prevent favouritism or ancient rivalries from interfering with political business. The policy is not universal; for some purposes a local person is more suitable.

The Kikuyu probably receive more than their share of prosperity; economic rivalry perceived as ethnic. Their dominance of entrepreneurial activities and land acquisition has created friction. First to receive tactical, token appointments to European-owned firms in the mid 1960s, Kikuyu received 45% of the land redistributed in the Million Acre Scheme. But on the other hand, thousands of Kikuyu farm labourers were displaced by Kalenjin-speaking and Kisii people who were resettled on the Rift Valley's formerly European farms. These latter groups also received the most fertile land and the most in proportion to population size and needs. When the Kenya National Trading Corporation gave out franchises for distribution rights for certain commodities there were claims among Kikuyu from Nyeri and Muran'ga that Kiambu Kikuyu were favoured. Government loans have been granted to Kikuyu enterprises in greater proportion than their numbers justify.

Immediately after taking office in 1978, President Moi suspended allocation of government land, so that the process could be regularised. That large holdings were not also broken up caused criticism, but from the point of view of stability, this hesitation may be wise. In April 1979, Attorney-General Njonjo (in connection with the prosecution of Kalenjin Enterprises Limited) said that all tribal names would be removed from companies.

Kikuyu regions have been privileged in primary and secondary school enrolment, national housing expenditure, and (with the

Costal region) provision of hospitals and doctors. Superior education is often cited as a reason for Kikuyu eminence in business and government. Research in fact suggests that there is no actual correlation between their level of education and business success. The Kikuyu lead in education is partly attributable to their own local investment and self-help "Harambee" secondary education. While the Luo provide a larger number of real scholars and writers, the Kikuyu have held top administrative and faculty positions at the University, and students from Central Province — Kikuyu — are also disproportionally represented there (as is the Kilimanjaro, Chagga region in Tanzania).

Both countries are now attempting to alleviate regional inequalities in education. Each utilises self-help in school provision, but wealthy and influential areas have maintained their lead. In 1974 free education was introduced in Kenya for the first 4 grades; enrolment increased considerably, and increased financial support to deprived regions was implemented. But Kenya, unlike Tanzania, did not allocate its best teachers to its most needy areas, and made no use of its schools for promoting a spirit of national service to replace regional competition.

In theory, Tanzania introduced universal primary education in 1977. In reality, from the lack of a school buildings, or the nomadic lives of some groups, it is not universal. But adult education has prospered. A national literacy campaign brought classes to more than 5 million out of 7½ million adults — in 5 years. Status attached to education is enhanced by the repression of private enterprise as an alternative means of upward mobility.

In Tanzania the majority have been organised (sometimes forcibly) into collective villages, with shared agricultural and social services. A willingness to co-operate rather than ethnic identity are traits sought of a neighbour. The stated intention is to prevent ethnicity from being a factor in economic development. In the absence of a paramount tribe, this has led to relative harmony. Yet some of the very policies designed to be equitable must cause problems for groups which enjoy a privileged level of prosperity. The village programme affects some tribes — for example the cattle owning Sukuma — more than others. There is evidence of resistance to it among the Mbula, Hehe and Chagga, as well as the Masai, for whom Ujamaa would be an abandonment of a way of life. (Medical facilities have been denied in some areas to coerce the adoption of less traditional dress).

Neither Kenya nor Tanzania appears guilty of a groundless discriminatory policy towards any particular minority. The Masai in both societies are somewhat out of the mainstream of development, but largely by choice. Kenya's most notable minority are the Somali of the north eastern deserts. From 1963–1966 there was insurgency aimed at reunion with Somalia. In 1977–1978 during the Ogaden War, there was strong surveillance — some say harrassment — of Somali. They were required to register and produce Kenyan identity cards on demand. In October, 1977 12 Kenya Somali MPs pledged loyalty to Kenya, and some Somali have recently become army officers. Nevertheless, the suspicion lingers that most Somalis would prefer to be citizens of an extended Somalia.

Other pastoral groups such as the Pokot, rivals of the Turkana for grazing land and water in the north, have been neglected until recently. There is embarrassment in sophisticated Nairobi over these "tourist attraction people": research is discouraged among them, unless it is development-orientated, exchanging the pastoral life to a stable and containable agricultural one. At the same time they are defenceless — and undefended — against banditry in the difficult border terrain. There have been reports that some stock bandits have received tacit police support — and were even intended to be involved in an assassination attempt on Moi, who is now expected to force all pastoralists to submit to education and "modernisation"; to what degree remains to be seen.

A new phase in "racial bargaining" has opened in Kenya with the election of Daniel Arap Moi as President. As Kenya's competitive society could ferment an "every tribe for itself" atmosphere, measures to counterbalance competitive pressures and old resentments must be particularly sensitive.

Kenya will have an uphill battle. The colonial heritage of Kikuyu and Luo dominance has been toyed with rather than attacked. The privileges of Kenyatta's family, clan, and inner cabinet were unjust. Yet while Kikuyu prominence must be reduced in the interests of fairness and stability, new and more vicious resentments must not be sparked off. The prosperity of the elite promotes the defence of its privileges, vested interests which are a factor in the alliance vying for post-Kenyatta power.

Although Moi did not change the Cabinet significantly, integration of minority opponents into the establishment (and selective coercion of disruptive elements) proved stabilising before the General Election of 1979. The privileged tend to respond only with complaints, and a trend, which may be healthy for Kenya, is the shift of leaders from claiming the right to rule as the providers of independence (Kikuyu in Mau Mau) to that of being the instruments of economic development. The appointment of Mwai Kibaki, a young very able Nyeri-based Kikuyu, as Vice President is an indication of this trend. The results of the General Election, however, again showed a rejection of Moi-supported Luo candidates in favour of Odinga's supporters. Odinga himself had been barred again from standing for election, and from the Chairmanship of KANU to which he aspired, although he has been compensated since with a senior statutory appointment.

Tanzania and Kenya are very different nations — the latter with far greater natural resources — operating opposing methods of economic development. Tanzania faces an economic crisis, largely exacerbated by the invasion of Uganda to rid the world of Amin, and from a refusal to comply with IMF regulations for loans, which it feels would undermine the consistency of its egalitarian economy. External commentators often compare these countries in order to promote their own ideologies: laissez-faire in Kenya, with apologies for corruption; socialism in Tanzania, avoiding both the instabilities and benefits of foreign investment and consequently "growing" more slowly. These commentators disregard the potential stimulus or drag of ethnic composition and competition on the development of a nation. Social policies, avowedly similar, have been applied in contrasting ways in Kenya and Tanzania; the application of these is behind the very reasoning for their political and economic policies.

Allan McChesney

BIBLIOGRAPHY

Areus, W., "Tribalism and the Poly-Ethnic Rural Community", 8 *Man* 441, 1973
Bienen, H., *Kenya: The Politics of Participation and Control,* Princeton University Press, Princeton N.J., 1974
Court, D., *Education as Social Control: The Response to Ine-*

quality in Kenya and Tanzania, Institute for Development Studies, University of Nairobi, 1975

Glickman, H., "Traditional Pluralism and Democratic Processes in Mainland Tanzania", *Asian and African Studies* 165, 1969

Legum, C., *Africa Contemporary Record 1977–78*, Africana Press, New York 1979

Meisler, S., "Tribal Politics Harass Kenya", 49 *Foreign Affairs* III, 1970

McChesney, R.A., *The Balance of Human Rights in Kenya and Tanzania*, University of London L.L.M. Paper (unpublished), London, 1978–79

Nellis, J.R., *Ethnic Composition of Leading Kenyan Government Positions*, The Scandinavian Institute of African Studies, Uppsala, 1974

31   The San of Botswana

The San, most commonly known as Bushmen, are one of the largest of the twenty-eight or so surviving hunter-gatherer societies in the world today. Once the sole and numerous inhabitants of all southern Africa, their number is now confined to the semi-arid Kalahari Desert. Two-thirds of the Kalahari falls within the geographic boundaries of the modern Republic of Botswana, and it is there that over half of the estimated 60,000 surviving San live, where they comprise nevertheless under 6% of that country's total population. An estimated 21,000 live in adjacent Namibia and 6,000 in southern Angola.

The inhospitable nature of the waterless Kalahari protected these people from the contact and persistent assimilation that met San in more fertile regions at each wave of Bantu migration into southern Africa, and their virtual extermination after the much later European settlement and expansion between 1652 and 1880. The Kalahari San were not to escape entirely, however; Tswana Bantu, fleeing west from the conflicts in the south, were gradually forced to settle on the fringes of the Kalahari region (1720–1880).

The early contact the Tswana cattle-owning people had with the Kalahari San was essentially peaceful, if exploitive; the Tswana used the San to hunt the abundant Kalahari wildlife and to provide precious ivory, skins and ostrich feathers. As they increased and expanded their occupation, however, the sources of livelihood for the San proportionately diminished; water sources, however remote, were pre-empted, game became scarce and important wildfoods eliminated as the fragile soil of the Kalahari was damaged by livestock. More and more hunting-and-gathering territories of the different San bands gave way to villages and cattle-posts, and affected San were forced or encouraged to eke a subsistence herding the Tswanas' ever-expanding cattle-herds. Whole bands were fragmented, and in time families came to be "owned" by leading tribesmen; in some areas their children were sold. As peaceful, recent, and necessarily gradual and scattered as the pastoral occupation of Botswana thus was, it was nevertheless effective in dispossessing and subjugating all but the most remote San. Throughout, the Tswana saw themselves as the benefactors of the primitive hunters, incorporating them as serfs in what they saw as their more advanced society.

Establishing a Protectorate (Bechuanaland) over the area in 1885, the British Government endorsed this relationship by failing to include the San in the division of the territory amongst the different tribes which gave them exclusive rights. The Colonial Government even proceeded to sell off the best land of previously uncontacted San in the far west (Ghanzi, 1898–1959). Only those groups of San in the most remote and marginal lands of the Desert were able to continue living by the unique mode of hunting-and-gathering, evolved over hundreds of years and adapted to the harsh Kalahari. Later with the advancing water technology of the twentieth century, many of these areas were opened up for livestock-grazing and yet more San displaced. By the 1960s only about 10,000, or less than a third of all San, were still hunting-and-gathering as their main source of subsistence. The remainder were caught in varying degrees of dependence and subservience to large cattle-owners, as herders, seasonal squatters, village serfs, and beggars; their circumstances increasingly characterised by poverty, apathy, social breakdown and demoralisation. The majority of even these San nevertheless tried to hunt and gather where they could, to supplement their meagre existence.

In 1966 Botswana gained independence from Britain and the racially distinct San became full and equal citizens of the new nation-state along with all the different Bantu tribesmen. This fact did not, however, radically alter their status, and they remain today as firmly entrenched as ever as the poorest and most exploited socio-economic sector of the still highly stratified rural society despite the Bushmen Development Programme of the new Government in 1974, specially designed to "foster their self-reliance and integration with the wider society". Under this Programme, the critical issues of land, water and hunting rights were tackled to some extent, and basic health, education and other services partially expanded to the cattle-posts and remote areas where they live. Water development as a means of securing San title to still unclaimed lands, and to enable those San still hunting-and-gathering to remain in their traditional lands proved important, as did plans to promote their hunting activity as a viable source of income.

However the Programme has never enjoyed popular, or serious political support; the Tswana having long regarded the minority San as primitives whose greatest need is to settle in villages where they may become "civilised" agriculturalists. Hunting-and-gathering is still not widely viewed as a viable use of land, and San who neither cultivate nor own livestock are not generally seen as requiring land. Their rights within the designated territories of the other tribes remain unclear, and post-Independence land law (1968) and policy (1971, 1973, 1975) has consistently failed to take account of this problem. Today, as the scarcity of land has become real, there is a marked reluctance to honour the commitments already made, and the appropriation of further San lands for the wealthier cattle-owning tribesmen is imminent — despite Botswana's much-proclaimed principle of national social justice.

There is an equal reluctance to see the introduction of legislation for minimum agricultural labour wages, such a move being viewed as upsetting the traditional and still current feudal relationship between San and large cattle-owners. Restrictive legislation passed in the sixties (1967–1971) continues to restrain San hunting, despite efforts to liberalise the regulations. On a wider front San are disadvantaged by their physical remoteness from the villages through which the Government channels the bulk of its rural development projects. As Botswana, a self-proclaimed non-racial state, becomes increasingly wary of its proximity to the Republic of South Africa and the implications of that country's reviled policies of Separate Development, so the unwillingness to make any concessions to the ethnic identity, unique way of life, or recent history of the San, hardens. Already San children, for example, may not be taught in their own languages, and pressure for the village settlement and total assimilation of the San into Tswana society, on the terms of the latter is growing. In 1978 The Bushmen Development Programme itself was absorbed into a more amorphous remote areas programme, its content reduced to welfare action, and the critical politicising role it had adopted, much subdued.

The outlook for San is bleak. Widely scattered, illiterate, often ignorant of important procedures and their rights as citizens, and without leaders of their own, San continue to lack the cohesion necessary to present a political voice on their own behalf, and are otherwise largely unrepresented in the national and local democratic institutions. Meanwhile official policy towards this minority is determinedly paternalist — wishing to see San advancement but not to an extent that might disrupt the present order however inherently inegalitarian it is. Without radical transformation of Botswana society, San will remain on its lowest rung.

Elizabeth Wily

BIBLIOGRAPHY

Childers, G., *Report of the Ghanzi Farms Basarwa (San) Investigation-Liaison Project*, Ministry of Local Govt and Lands, Gabarone, 1976

Lee, R.B., and Irven de Vore, *Kalahari Hunter-Gatherers: Studies of the Kun San and Their Neighbours*, Harvard University Press, Mass., 1976

London Missionary Society, *The Masarwa (Bushmen): Report of An Inquiry by the South Africa District Committee of the London Missionary Society*, Lovedal Press, 1935

Republic of Botswana, *Minutes of the Remote Area Development Programme Workshop held at BTC 29 May–2 June 1978*, Government Printer, Gabarone, 1978

Republic of Botswana, *Third National Development Plan of Botswana 1975/8*, Government Printer, Gabarone, 1975

Silberhauser, G.B., *Report to the Bechuanaland Protectorate on the Bushman Survey*, Government Printer, Gabarone, 1965

Sillery, A., *Botswana: A Short Political History*, Methuen, London 1974

Tagart, E.S.B., *Report of the Conditions Existing Among the Masarwa in the Bamangwatoo Reserve of the Bechuanaland Protectorate and Certain Other Matters Appertaining to the Natives Living Therein*, Government Printer, Pretoria, 1933

32   The Scottish Gaels

According to the 1971 Census there were 88,415 persons aged three or over in Scotland able to speak Gaelic and English, and 477 persons able to speak Gaelic only. The combined total of 88,892 represented a percentage of 1.8 of the population of Scotland (aged three and over). The 1961 total had been 80,978, but all previous Census returns since 1891 had shown a decline in the number of Gaelic speakers.

The largest concentrations of Gaelic speakers are in Ross and Cromarty (18,510), Inverness County (18,740) and Glasgow City (12,865). Local Government reorganisation has redefined the two first-mentioned areas, and now the Western Isles Region coincides with the greatest concentration of Gaelic speech. In 1971 Lewis (Landward) was 89.6% Gaelic-speaking, North Uist 89.2, Harris 88.8, Barra 87.3, South Uist 77.2. Other places showing high percentages were Skye (66.9), Tiree and Coll (66.7), Islay (51.2) and Lochcarron (50.7). The latter is the only mainland district so far referred to. Gaelic speech is fairly strong in parts of Wester Ross and West Sutherland (e.g. Applecross and Durness) and in pockets in West Inverness-shire and Ardamurchan, but these places are sparsely populated. Gaelic speakers are to be found in virtually every Scottish community, but in most they are in a tiny minority. Stornoway has the largest Gaelic percentage (53.7) for a town, and there are significant numbers of Gaelic in Glasgow, Edinburgh, Inverness, Aberdeen, Oban and other towns.

There has been a marked revival of interest in Gaelic in recent decades, resulting in a large following for the National Mod (Music and Language festival) and for radio and TV Gaelic programmes, and a wide proliferation of Gaelic classes. This revival clearly has links with the political movement for Scottish independence, but no formal connections.

Gaelic has declined from being the dominant language in Scotland (9th to 13th centuries), and in the course of its decline has suffered some active repression. The Statutes of Iona (1609) and Privy Council enactments of 1616 sought to direct the families of chiefs towards English schooling in the Lowlands. Political measures especially after the '45 attacked Highland culture. In the first half of the eighteenth century the Society for the Propagation of Christian Knowledge thought it advisable to eradicate Gaelic and Popery (twin evils), and the 1872 Education Act (Scotland) appeared to judge Gaelic irrelevant to education. As a result of these historical and official attitudes, Gaelic has a very precarious standing still: it is not used in the courts, it is used very sparingly in public signs and notices, there is little tradition of using it in public business (apart from the Churches), and its position in schools, and in the media has to be constantly fought for. Official attitudes are, in the main, no longer repressive, but small encouragements are regarded as generous, and there is little governmental initiative exercised. The Western Isles Region has an official bilingual policy, which is being gradually and selectively implemented in schools and in public business, but a more positive Scottish policy is needed for example, ensuring, equal validity for Gaelic and English, the use of Gaelic in a range of public documents and notices, the development of various registers of Gaelic, more adequate funding for publications and for work in the media, and further development of many kinds in education, from the publication of more books for children to the active encouragement of post-graduate research of Gaelic topics.

The political climate seems better for Gaelic than it has been for hundreds of years. The Scottish National Party has published a comprehensive Gaelic policy, and all the other Scottish political parties have subsequently made pronouncements about Gaelic. Scottish independence would undoubtedly boost support for Gaelic, but the outlook is not unpromising otherwise. It may be that the EEC dimension will favour a more open, less insular, attitude to minority languages and cultures, and world-wide interest in submerged and underdeveloped groupings will perhaps exert similar pressure.

In the course of the twentieth century the position of Gaelic in Scottish life has been steadily improved by the action of dedicated Gaels. "An Comunn Gaidhealach" (The Highland Association) was founded in 1891 and has intermittently acted as an important pressure-group, helping to re-establish Gaelic in the educational system for example. This has been achieved at many levels; the three main gaps are: the use of Gaelic as the primary language of literacy in the Gaelic area; the use of Gaelic as a medium of instruction in upper primary and in secondary schools (also in the Gaelic area); and the extension of modest Gaelic-teaching facilities elsewhere in Scotland. Gaelic is well-established in radio, and has a foothold in TV; both need considerable development, in time and range. The foundation of the Scottish Gaelic Texts Society in the 1930s has led to a succession of definitive publications of the work of poets and prose-writers. Gaelic publishing has had a useful revival of its own since the 1960s, with Gairm Publications forming the spearhead, and the Gaelic Books Council (from 1968) providing financial and other aid, mainly with funds from the Scottish Education Department and the Scottish Arts Council. Gaelic poetry has currently something of an international reputation, while drama is likely to derive great encouragement from the recent founding of a Gaelic Repertory Theatre. Academic work on dialects, lexicography and folklore has been proceeding for some time, but still needs additional funding. A programme of language development is being spasmodically implemented, but requires more specific planning and funding.

In summary, the objectives for advance have been fairly well defined, the political climate for that advance seems possible if not actively propitious, and it is to be hoped that positive encouragement will not be too late to arrest and reverse the long decline of Gaelic speech in Scotland.

Derick S. Thomson

BIBLIOGRAPHY

Gaelic Books Council, *A Catalogue of Gaelic Books in Print*, University of Glasgow
Scottish Nationalist Party, 'A' Ghaidhlig: na tha romhainn a dheanamh' (SNP Gaelic policy), in *Gairm*, 104 Sept, 1978 Gaor, Publications Glasgow (English version from S.N.P.)
Campbell, J.L., *Gaelic in Scottish Education and Life*, W. and A.K. Johnston for the Saltire Society Edinburgh 1950
Grimble, I. and Thomson, D.S., *The Future of the Highlands*, Routledge and Kegan Paul, London, 1968
Mackinnon, Kenneth, *The Lions Tongue*, Club Leabhar, Inverness, 1974
Thomson, D.S., *Gaelic in Scotland*, Gairm Publications, Glasgow, 1976
Thomson, D.S., *An Introduction to Gaelic Poetry*, Gollancz, London, 1974

33   Sikh Immigrants in England

Approximately one half of the estimated 1.3 million South Asians in Great Britain have peasant origins from the state of Punjab, India, and adhere to the Sikh religion. By migrating to England, they have aided in the economic advancement of themselves, of Punjab, and of Britain. Despite their contributions, these Asians are increasingly becoming the targets of racial resentment for, unlike their West Indian counterparts, their numbers in Britain continue to increase. According to Great Britain's 1971 Census, 322,670 inhabitants were originally born in India and 126,455 claim Pakistan or Bangladesh as their origin. However considering those born in England of South Asian parentage, arrivals since the Census and others claiming Indian or Pakistani identity, the present numbers are estimated as above.

Indians and their Punjabi Sikh segment have been part of the

British scene for over a hundred years. At the end of World War II there were about 5,000 South Asians in Britain and their numbers were soon to mushroom, as England needed labourers for its post-war industrial recovery, while Punjab's resources were severely taxed as a result of partition and the influx of Hindu and Sikh refugees from the creation of Muslim Pakistan in 1947. In Punjab, newspaper articles, gossip, letters from England, and travel agents portrayed the British Isles as a land of easy and unlimited wealth. Believing these exaggerated tales, loans were obtained, and kin groups pooled resources to send capable males to England to make a future, help other kinsmen migrate and then rejoin their wives, children, and friends in Punjab as prosperous and important men.

New arrivals in the 1950s were generally helped by their countrymen already established in England. There was a comradely spirit in these early years. Even though these Sikhs lived in sparse and over-crowded dwellings (sometimes there were over thirty men in a three bedroomed house), they shared what they had and sent over half of their earnings back to India, thus bringing prosperity to the "sending" community. These Asians quickly earned the reputation of being good workers and provided needed unskilled manpower for vacancies in British firms. But since many of these new-comers did not know British ways, they fell victim to exploitive bilingual brokers (usually Asian) who acted as "advisers", finding the Sikh a job and then taking an excessive portion from each pay packet. Some Indians did not even know the wage they were supposed to receive, and if they complained, they feared being put in jail or losing everything.

Initially the receiving society ignored these dark-skinned labourers for they remained apart, within their own ghettos; a proud people with little desire to become part of the wider community. With the 1958 Notting Hill race riots and immigration increasing to 34,410 annually by 1959, public concern increased. By 1960, Punjabi Sikhs and other immigrants feared that controls would be implemented to restrict future inflows, and so wives, children, relatives, and friends were sponsored by Punjabis in England to migrate, but they too felt that the sojourn would be short. More villagers arrived, causing the explosive situation that the restrictionalists had hoped to avoid.

With the reuniting of families, the Punjabi Sikh communities in England established principles that guide their actions today.

Village cultural values were reinstituted and men no longer had the freedom that they had experienced earlier, for now they had to consider their honour (*izzat*) and the future of their kinsmen in India. Yet the Sikhs also had to deal with English institutions, particularly schools, which taught, *inter alia*, that certain Asian customs, like arranged marriages, were archaic and inhuman. While the British educational system is culturally Eurocentric, many Punjabis perceived English co-education as immoral, preferring a "Victorian" arrangement of sex separation. At the same time the host society, especially its lower classes, felt threatened by the continued arrival of more Indians, especially since the formation of ghettos, where their distinctive manners and clothes made them conspicuous.

Sikh kin groups organised to maximise their assets. Joint residence minimised expenses; men worked unbelievably hard, logging up to 90 hours per week. Every available male or female had a job; generally an elderly grandmother or teenage female tended the small children. As soon as possible boys and girls left school to join their parents in the factories. As one lady explained in 1970: "All Parliament has to do is pass a law and we will have to leave. We must earn as fast as we can now." Although many did not experience direct discrimination, gossip, the pronouncements of politicians, newspaper reports of clashes and a racially hostile atmosphere has made the Indians in England feel insecure.

Gurdwaras, Sikh places of worship, sprang up and became the social centre for the Indians, although men also continued to value the pub as a place to meet friends. *Gurdwara* committees became the representatives of the Punjabis to the host community, and although they remained largely hidden from public view, political groups were formed. These "parties" as the Punjabis termed them, functioned as social agencies to help their members deal with British shop-keeping and bureaucracy. They also organised quietly to protect their members against blackmail, extortion, exploitation and physical attack. They are a strong force in political competition, whether it is for the chairmanship of an Indian organisation or supporting a parliamentary candidate in an election. (All Commonwealth citizens resident in the U.K. have the right to vote.)

Despite the 1968 Immigration Act restricting numbers, from 1970 onwards, Punjabi migrants in Britain began to realise they would not be returning to their villages. They now became concerned about preserving Sikh culture in Britain, for their young learned Western ideas in school that often contradicted the views of their elders. Parents pressed for early marriage, with spouses from Punjabi villages being preferred, fearing that in Britain their daughters would lose their virginity and their sons marry white girls. This has caused emotional traumas among Sikh children, particularly girls raised in England, for village concepts of marriage and the status of women differ greatly from those of the Sikh influenced by British culture.

Today, for the second generation males, advancement in education and training in such fields as medical science, engineering and accountancy — skills that can be used in both India and England — have begun to take precedence over factory work. Education is perceived as a key to social advancement. Punjabi Sikh villagers will be a part of Britain's society for a long time, but will for the immediate future maintain themselves in an enclave. The hearts of the first generation villagers are still in India. For the second generation in England, while they are present physically, emotionally they belong neither in India or England. They are often rejected by the English community, yet they cannot adhere fully to the teachings of their fathers.

Arthur W. Helweg

BIBLIOGRAPHY

Aurora, G.S., *The New Frontiersmen*, Popular Prakshan, Bombay, 1967

Ballard, R., "Family Organisation among the Sikhs in Britain", in *New Community*, Vol 2, No 1, 1972–3

Desai, R., *Indian Immigrants in Britain*, Oxford University Press for the Institute of Race Relations, 1963

Helweg, A., "Punjabi Farmers: Twenty Years in England", in *India International Centre Quarterly*, Vol 5, No 1, 1978

Hiro, D. *The Indian Family in Britain*, Community Relations Commission, London, Revised 1972

Hames, A., *Sikh Children in Britain*, Oxford University Press for the Institute of Race Relations, London, 1974

Kohler, D. *Ethnic Minorities in Britain: Statistical Data*, Community Relations Commission, London, 1976

Sharma, U. *Rampal and His Family*, Collins, London 1971
Tinker, H. *The Banyan Tree; Overseas Immigrants from India, Pakistan and Bangladesh*, Oxford University Press, 1977
Wilson, A., *Finding a Voice: Asian Women in Britain*, Virago, London, 1978

34   The South Tyroleans

The South Tyrol, known in Italian as the province of Bolzano, and to its German-speaking inhabitants as *Südtirol*, is situated in Italy's northernmost region of Trentino-Alto Adige, on the border with Austria. Here, according to the Census of 1971, live approximately 260,000 people whose mother-tongue is German. The total population of the region in 1971 was 433,215 and its area is 2,815 square miles, the principal towns being Bolzano and Merano.

For fourteen centuries a part of the German-speaking world, the South Tyrol has been the territory of the Italian State only since 1919 and the Treaty of St. Germain. During the Middle Ages the area was one of the brightest jewels in the Habsburg crown, its people developing a strong, independent character based on local customs and liberties, and their own systems of democratic government, which they defended against threats of Franco-Bavarian dominations. On the eve of World War I, the population of the South Tyrol consisted of approximately 232,700 German-speakers and Ladin-speakers, 7,100 Italian-speakers and 11,700 people of other language groups. It was essentially a rural region, dependent on the cultivation of vines and fruits in the valleys and stock rearing, forestry and farming in the mountains. The people were mostly farmers, literate in German and deeply Catholic, an ethnically homogeneous community passionately attached to their land and way of life, conservative and naturally suspicious of the *italianata* to the South.

Italy was drawn into the war on the side of France and Britain after they had promised that, in the event of their victory, South Tyrol (and the Istria peninsula) would be given to the Italians, and the Peace Conference of 1919 recognised Italy's claims. At the collapse of Austria-Hungary, Italian troops were installed on the Brenner Pass where they were able to deal with resistance from the *Schützen*, the people's militia of the South Tyrol. The annexation of the area was widely resented in Austria but most bitterly felt by the South Tyroleans themselves. Unprotected by any minority treaty, they quickly lost faith in the Rome Government's promises to respect their individuality. To the subtle process of cultural assimilation was added outright oppression by the Fascist authorities. German was proscribed from public life and officials were replaced by Italians; the name *Südtirol* was officially changed to Alto Adige, political parties and unions were disbanded, all personal names Italianised, as were the schools, and there was determined repression of anything which might remind the people of their German past. South Tyroleans were evicted from their land and replaced by Italians and employment in the factories around Bolzano was reserved for the Italians. Within a few years the South Tyroleans were relegated to a position of economic and social inferiority, withdrawing from the towns where there was little work for them and falling back on the mountains for their livelihood. The South Tyroleans reverted to being a principally peasant people. By 1939 85,600 Italians were living on South Tyrol forming a quarter of the population.

The 'Pact of Steel' between Mussolini and Hitler had an even more devastating effect on the process of assimilation: on 26 June 1939 an agreement was signed in Berlin providing for the transference of the South Tyrol's entire population from Italy to the German Reich. The people had a choice between complete denationalisation with the prospect of deportation to other parts of Italy, or transference to the Reich with their ethnic identity preserved. Faced with such an alternative, and under most crude pressure from both sides, the South Tyroleans opted for the Reich: 183,365 out of 266,885 chose this fate. In the event, the transference was obstructed by the war but, nevertheless, by the end of 1943 some 75,000 people had been moved, most were town-dwellers and officials with only a small percentage of farmers. A decree offered repatriation to Italy in 1948 but only a third took advantage of it.

Following the defeat of Fascism in 1944, the South Tyrol was handed back to Italy; Austria protested in vain. The 1946 Paris Peace Conference Agreement was meant to close the controversy over to whom the South Tyrol would belong. Placed under an international regime, with Austria in a supervisory role, the South Tyroleans found themselves in a new situation. According to the Agreement primary and secondary education in German were to be guaranteed, parity between German and Italian restored and the German forms of surnames allowed. The South Tyrol's wish for regional autonomy was conceded in Article II with the exercise of legislative and executive powers. This was intended to compensate for the fundamentally weak position of South Tyroleans compared with that of the Italian-speaking majority. However, until up to 1969 regional autonomy was granted, not to the South Tyrol as a single administrative unit, but to the Region of Trentino-Alto Adige — a much larger area in which Italians are in the majority. The province of Bolzano and Trento did have considerable powers with fairly autonomous executives, but it was a limited arrangement beset with problems. Folk culture and education rested with the provinces while responsibility for economic development belonged to the Region, delegating its administrative functions reluctantly, slowly and in a spirit increasingly hostile to the Statute of Autonomy. The Rome Government and its centralist administration did the rest: autonomy in the South Tyrol fell far short of the terms of the Paris Agreement, except in the sphere of language education. (In the province of Bolzano teaching up to the age of 18 was in the mother tongue.)

This failure to implement, in practice, the Paris Agreement caused the German-speaking population of the South Tyrol, after years of delay, to feel itself threatened as a community. The increasing immigration of Italians, encouraged by industrialists and by systematic discrimination in the allocation of housing, exacerbated the situation. Many thousands of South Tyroleans migrated to Switzerland, Austria and West Germany, especially to the industrial conurbations of the Ruhr. The region's standard of living has improved during the last twenty years, but with almost complete Italianisation of the main towns and valley. Whereas in 1910 about 97% of the South Tyrol's population was German-speaking, by 1945 the percentage had fallen to 66%; by

1961 their numbers had dropped again to 232,717 (62%), living for the most part outside the towns.

The South Tyroleans' profound feeling of resentment has been expressed principally through the *Südtiroler Volkspartei*, a party which in 1954 formally asked the Italian Government for the full application of the Statute of Autonomy. When no reply was received, a number of incidents, demonstrations and later attacks on Government property took place. On Herz Jesu Nacht 1959 there were no less than 47 explosions in the province, in which one person was killed. The dispute increased in intensity and complexity during the 1960s, becoming more and more litiginous and diplomatic as both the Austrian and the Italian Governments tried to avoid it, each as intransigent as the other. Terrorism increased, Italy vetoed commercial negotiations between Austria and the EEC and the South Tyrolean problem remained unsolved.

Eventually an agreement was reached at Copenhagen in 1969. Italy agreed to add to the Statute of Autonomy a number of improvements, commonly known as 'The Package' to be applied over several years, including provision for the teaching of German at all levels of education and the training of teachers, a wider use of German in administration, the active encouragement of culture and the extension of political autonomy.

Relations between the Italian Government and the Region began to improve following this agreement. The majority of the South Tyroleans (87% in 1974) continued to support the *SVP*, and that party remained critical of 'The Package', claiming that the balance was still in favour of the Italian-speaking minority. The political unity of the South Tyroleans was ruptured in 1971, when the SVP divided into two equal camps, one following Dr. Silvius Magnago, the President, in his moderate, conciliatory attitude towards Rome, the other adopting a more hostile view.

The degree of autonomy granted to the South Tyrol by the Statute of 1972 was extensive within the context of the Italian State. Other than currency, taxes, foreign affairs and defence, the province of Bolzano has been granted full powers. Judges and civil servants must be appointed from among both linguistic groups, and about 5,000 posts are thus reserved for German-speakers. The German language has been accorded full official status with Italian, and all documents, signs and announcements must be in both. The Province also controls radio, television, cultural affairs and schools. There is, however, a very real danger that this autonomy will remain a "dead letter" if it is not implemented fully and soon. The *SVP*, which can claim almost exclusive responsibility for having created the new situation now seeks to ensure that the Statute becomes fully effective and maintained. It is still the majority party in the Provincial Assembly.

The South Tyroleans are in many ways typical of minorities which are separated from their ethnic homeland and incorporated in another State. The German-speakers, obliged to accept Italian citizenship in 1919 and again in 1945, learned that they were politically weak and had few institutions capable of attracting the central government's attention, while Italy herself fears that Alto Adige might be exploited by Austria. A new and integrated, but federal, Europe will require a bridge between the German and Italian worlds formed by the necessary economic and cultural stability of the multi-lingual community.

Meic Stephens

BIBLIOGRAPHY

Alcock, A.E., *The History of the South Tyrol Question* London, 1970

Bracolini, R., *L'ABC dell' Alto Adige*, Milano, 1968

Cajoli, Renato, *L'Autonomia del Trentino-Alto Adige*, Bologna, 1952

Carandini, N., *The Alto Adige, an experiment in the devaluation of frontiers*, Rome, 1958

Czikann-Sichy, M., *Turmoil in South Tyrol*, New York, 1960

Finet, A., *La Question du Tyrol du Sud*, Paris, 1968

Hermes, Peter, *Die sudtiroler Autonomie*, Frankfurt, 1952

Pontali, A., *Negotiations and Dynamite*, Rome, 1963

Siegler, A., *The Problem of South Tyrol*, Vienna, 1959

35 Two Slave Descended Communities: Creoles of Sierra Leone and Afro-Americans in Liberia

Sierra Leone was first explored by Pedro da Cintra, a Portuguese officer who visited the coastal area in 1460 and named the mountainous peninsula at the mouth of the Rokel River "Serra Lyoa" (Lion Mountain) from where the country gained its name. The region's main export between the 16th and early 18th centuries was slaves. In 1787 a group of abolitionists, based in London founded Freetown as a resettlement centre for freed slaves from Britain and the West Indies. The abolitionists, naturally, could not participate in the current export economy, so the settlement, therefore, had to be supported by annual grants-in-aid from the British government. It consequently became a crown colony in 1808 and the interior became a British protectorate in 1896.

The Creole community amounts to no more than 3% of Sierra Leone's 3 million dense population. They are almost all Christians and culturally have combined traditions from Britain and the West Indies with those of the indigenous tribal population. They speak English, the official language, or *Krio*, the lingua franca. It was they who went as missionaries into the hinterland where Christianity became blended with animist beliefs. They have formed the nation's elite intellectual circles and have some influence in the economy, but their dominance has never compared with that of Afro-Americans in neighbouring Liberia.

In 1816 the American Colonisation Society was founded to return freed black slaves to their ancestral West African homeland. It was to be a humanitarian answer to the problem of how freed slaves, in pre-official emancipation days, should live, and to prevent them from being re-enslaved by unscrupulous dealers.

By 1822, the first group arrived and established a "colony" on Providence Island, which had been purchased by the Society a year earlier. Two years later the colony was named "Liberia", and the main settlement "Monrovia", in honour of American president James Monroe. By 1847 the Virginia-born governor of Liberia, Joseph Jenkins Roberts, proclaimed Liberia an independent republic — the first in Africa — a move not recognised by the United States government until 1862. In the following years the Liberian republic lost territory to neighbouring British and French colonies and through poor financial management the economic superstructure nearly collapsed several times in the late 19th and early 20th centuries. The descendants of the freed American slaves, who had dominated the country from the start, began to develop the economy. Firestone Tire and Rubber Company obtained a 1 million acre concession for rubber plantations in 1926 and began the exploitation of Liberian rubber. Eventually other plantations were opened, iron ore and diamonds were discovered, and Liberia became a "flag of convenience" for the world shipping industry, particularly for tankers. The slave descendants still dominate the economic, political and social institutions of Liberia in spite of the relative size of their group.

The indigenous population is based on three language groups; West Atlantic, Mande and Kru. The West Atlantic group includes the Kissi and Gola tribes found mainly in the mountainous north and west; the Mande group composed of the Vai (who developed an alphabet in the 19th century, later used by the Germans in World War II as a code), Mano, Kpelle and Dan tribes, located in central Liberia, and the militant Kru group, which includes the Kru (the largest tribe in Liberia) and Bassa tribes who inhabit the coast and the south, on the border with the Ivory Coast. The indigenous population are largely found as plantation labourers, mine workers and domestic servants, or in subsistence farming. Although some tribes have been converted to either Christianity or Islam, 80% remain animist.

The slave-descended community accounts for about 2.5% of the population and they have been a pervasive cultural influence in Liberia. The similarities between Liberia today and the United States at the turn of the century are remarkable. The U.S. dollar is the principal currency used. The Liberian flag is a one star version of the American flag. A fifth of the population speak

English as their first language, which is also the lingua franca. Place names such as Harper, Robertsport, Greenville, Maryland, Buchanan and Brewerville illustrate American influence. The Constitutional division between executive, legislative and judiciary are based on the U.S. system. The Afro-American community is Christian and "middle class".

In Sierra Leone, two groups, the Mande and West Atlantic predominate; the Mande includes the Mende, Dyalonke, Koranko and Vai; the West Atlantic group includes the Temne, Kissi and Bullom. Other smaller tribes include the Mandingo and Peul. The Temne and the Mende each make up one third of the national population. Animism is still prominent although various forms of Christianity exist, while a third of the national population is classified as Muslim, notably the Peul (or Fulani).

Under British rule, the Creole community prospered. The capital, Freetown developed as a major trading port (especially before the building of the Suez Canal, though it has remained important for trade with Africa and South America) and as the base for the rescue for slave cargoes. It became the seat of the first institution of higher learning in black Africa — Fourah Bay College — the source of education for the Creoles, and Africans from all over the continent. The British were careful not to allow the Creole community to dominate colonial politics. The 1924 constitution brought the tribal chiefs of the protectorate into the legislative council and by 1943 Africans were admitted to the executive council for the first time (both products of a persistent belief in indirect rule). Neither of these developments satisfied the rising demands of nationalist movements, but they did ensure tribal participation in future political and constitutional settlements. The 1951 Constitution established the framework for independence (which came ten years later) papering over the differences between Creole education and wealth, and the rest of the country. Sierra Leone started favourably with a stable government and apparently promising economic development centred on diamonds, iron ore, palm products, coffee and cocoa, but since independence, the nation has experienced political upheaval, nepotism, poor administration, corruption and tribal animosity. The exploitation of Sierra Leone's diamonds was entirely, and remains largely, in foreign hands, initially British, but to these were added Lebanese and Indian merchants. They provided little employment but encouraged individuals to give up agriculture in expectation of wealth and real economic development was slow.

The Creoles, due to their colonial importance as a professional group, are now the victims of much prejudice from the other groups. Their language, religion, occupations and culture are neither African nor truly British. Several governments have attempted to cope with this animosity, manifest in two decades of coups, counter-coups and political intrigue. As in Liberia, solutions can only lie in the breaking down of tribalism and the more equitable distribution of the nation's wealth. Sierra Leone can return to optimism only when her government deals with the serious ethnic divisions which have been the source of much prejudice and unrest.

Liberian politics suffer from an amazing lack of change. The major party, the True Whig Party (slave-descended) has held the reins of government continuously for the last 101 years, a record unequalled in the world. The last two presidents, William V.S. Tubman and William Tolbert, have no trace of indigenous blood. Their cabinets have been composed of no less than 58% slave descendants and usually about 75%, while the civil service and diplomatic corps are almost totally Afro-American. Nepotism and corruption are unwritten rules of Liberian politics.

In 1943, William V.S. Tubman promised to begin a programme of social development in order to speed the unification of the country. Improvements in agricultural techniques and the growth of foreign investment have, however, only indirectly benefited the indigenous peoples, and they remain outside the circles of economic, political and social leadership. The Afro-American community has surrounded itself with the legitimised, if borrowed, myths of Manifest Destiny and a civilising mission. They speak out against colonialism, but only their colour distinguishes them from the other colonisers of the African continent. A high degree of institutionalism along with the myth of civilisation enables the ruling elite to preserve their dominion and absorb the major dissenting indigenous leaders, when necessary, into the system. The only road to wealth, employment and status is through the existing political structure and the True Whig Party. Under Tolbert, the indigenous population of Liberia has been given a larger role in national affairs, but without concessions that would affect the interests or position of the ruling elite to any extent.

The government has also practised "divide and rule" policies amongst the various tribes and yet there is one area of importance in which the indigenous people have become dominant from sheer numbers — the armed forces. In 1973 two of the three generals were Lomas and many lower ranking officers were Kru (who have been the only source of opposition in the twentieth century). There have been several sporadic incidents of unrest in the military, but all have been quieted by either co-option or imprisonment. Under Tolbert, several tribal leaders were appointed to positions of responsibility in their home areas and several diplomats were appointed from some of the groups converted to Christianity, but there were no constitutional or legal changes to the advantage of the majority. While the indigenous population of Liberia is gradually gaining higher living standards, there is no commensurate increase in their political power. In the future, Liberia may prove the classical theory of a revolution of rising expectations. In a world increasingly more conscious of civil and political rights, a 2.5% minority will not find the retention of national power as easy as in the past. Nineteen Seventy-Nine saw the inauguration and sudden growth of a new opposition party: change lies ahead for Liberia.

R.F.

BIBLIOGRAPHY

Cartwight, John, *Political Leadership in Sierra Leone*, London, 1978

Clapham, Christopher, *Liberia and Sierra Leone*, Cambridge, 1976

Dunn, John, *West African States: Failure and Promise*, Cambridge, 1978

Porter, Arthur T., *Creoledom*, London, 1971

Kup, A.P., *Sierra Leone*, London, 1975

Price, J.H., *Political Institutions of West Africa*, London, 1967

Spitzer, Leo, *The Creoles of Sierra Leone*, Madison, Wisconsin, 1974

Liebenow, J.G., *Liberia: The Evolution of Privilege*, Cornell, 1969

36 The Swedes in Finland

For six centuries the Swedes ruled and colonised Finland. They invaded and converted Finland to Christianity in the early 12th century, and established small Swedish colonies on the coasts, trading in fur and amber with central Finland and Russia. When Sweden became a centralised state in the sixteenth century, Swedish became the language of authority and administration in Finland. After over a century of encroachment by the Russian Empire, Finland was ceded as a Grand Duchy to the Russians in 1809, the province of Vyborg having been acquired already by the Russians in 1721. Under Russian rule the Finns enjoyed a degree of autonomy, but the Russianisation programme of Czar Nicholas II evoked strong resistance from the growing Finnish nationalist movement. Eventually after several assassinations and a general strike, the Russians conceded, yielding greater autonomy to the Finns, establishing a unicameral Diet to replace the Four Estate Diet and introducing universal suffrage. At the outbreak of the Bolshevik Revolution the Finns, under Marshal Carl Gustav Mannerheim, broke away from Russia to establish a republic. A large number of Swedes and Swedish-speaking institutions remained; they had vied throughout the period of Russianisation to keep Swedish the language of education and intellectual life.

Today the Swedish-speaking population of Finland accounts for 6.5% of Finland's population of 4,700,000. They are found in three major areas of concentrations: the southern coast between Hango and Helsinki extending inland for about 50 miles and the western coast between Pori and Jakobstad, as well as the Ahvenanmaa or Åland (Aaland) Islands. Swedish groups are also found in Helsinki, Turku, Raahe and Oulu. Like the Finns, the Swedes are Lutherans and there is a Swedish diocese, Borga. Their culture and social institutions are close to those in Sweden.

Between 1900 and 1930 there was considerable emigration to the U.S.A. and Canada, reducing the proportion of the Swedish-speaking population from 12.89% to its present figure. Some 60,000 Finnish citizens of Swedish origin now live in Sweden. "Mixed" marriages, where the children take to the linguistic group of the majority, also causes some reduction. Most Swedes are bilingual, and are very much in demand for trade and tourist links with Sweden. The 1919 Constitution and decree of 1922 recognise both languages equally in courts and in towns where the minority rises above 8%. Since the linguistic conflict in the nineteenth century, there have been few language controversies, except over the State University of Helsinki, which gave instruction in Swedish until 1937. Today the constitutional status of the Swedes is regarded as exemplary.

The Aaland Islands form an archipelago of wooded islands off the south west coast of Finland, occupying a strategic position, wedged between the Gulf of Bothnia, the Gulf of Finland and the main body of the Baltic Sea, with the additional advantage of a position straddling the major trade routes leading to Turku, Stockholm, Helsinki, Tallinn, Leningrad and the northern ports of Sweden and Finland. The islands' population of 20,800 is totally Swedish-speaking and the archipelago itself lies nearer to Sweden than to Finland. The Finnish claim to the islands goes back to the time of the first Swedish invasions. Due to their strategic position, the islands were demilitarised in 1856 by a convention between France, Britain and Russia, and there is still no military service, unlike the mainland. Because of their ties with Sweden, the Aaland islanders sought to become part of Sweden when Finland gained its independence in 1917. Finland granted the islands autonomy in 1920 but refused to recognise the secession, a claim which the League of Nations supported in 1921. Disputes continued in the 1920s and 1930s when islanders went to the Swedish court with their grievances, but since World War II the Aaland Islands have posed few domestic problems for Finland. With a self-government Act passed in December 1951, the Aaland Islands remain autonomous with their own elected council, congress (*maakunta*) and "land councillor" (prime minister). However the provincial governor appointed by the Finnish government has veto powers over congressional decisions.

The Swedes on the mainland of Finland have in recent years

benefited from the establishment of communal self-government in which every commune in Finland conducts its own local affairs and determines its language status. Of 22 newspapers, eight are Swedish and there are five permanent Swedish theatres. Swedish political power is based on the Swedish People's Party (Svenska Folkpartiet i Finland or SFF). The SFF is a loose heterogenous structure, unusual in the Finnish political system, because it is the only party that does not fit a straight left-right continuum. The party supports the continued preservation of Swedish culture, but also offers a comprehensive national programme. It has many splinter groups and though it supports a free market economy and private property, its social policy tends to be socialist. The SFF usually polls about 142,000 votes out of 2,360,000, making it Finland's sixth largest party (out of eight) and a participant in many coalitions. About 16 out of 200 members of the Chamber of Deputies are Swedish, of whom over half are SFF. It has become common practice to include one or two Swedish-speaking ministers in the government.

With the vigilance of the SFF, the establishment of communal self-government and the special autonomy of the Aaland Islands, the Swedish-speaking community in Finland could perhaps be considered one of the best treated minorities in the world. Assisted by Finland's close relations with Sweden, the Swedish-Finns have both preserved their culture and integrated themselves into Finland's politics and society.

Randall Fegley

BIBLIOGRAPHY

Eskola, A., *Local Self-Government and Municipal Law in Finland*, Helsinki, 1968
Nickels, S. et al, *Finland: An Introduction*, London, 1973
Nousiainen, J., *The Finnish Political System*, Cambridge, Mass., 1971
Puntila, L.A., *The Political History of Finland 1809-1966*, London, 1975

37   The Welsh in Argentina

The idea of a Welsh settlement in Argentina derived from the demographic effects of the industrial revolution and the events in mid-century which affected the political philosophy of leaders in many different parts of Europe. By the 18th century the ruling class in Wales had become alienated, socially, economically and culturally, from the mass of the population; their affinity lay with members of the ruling class in England with whom they shared a common interest in reproducing the social and cultural order in Wales. This was further entrenched with the advent of the industrial revolution which was financed from outside Wales and controlled by non-Welsh personnel. In mid-century there were many Welsh leaders who focused attention on the resultant cultural division of labour. Such leaders were often non-conformists who eventually aligned with the Liberal party and emphasised the Welsh language in opposition to the English speaking Tories who patronised the Church of England. The issues which derived from this polarisation included land nationalisation, enfranchisement, religious freedom, language freedom and educational opportunity. Many of these ideas were rooted in a form of socialism which derived from Chartism and even the early works of Marx as well as the writings of various European nationalists including Kosuth, Mazini and Davis.

The number of Welsh people emigrating from Wales increased, a considerable number of them leaving for North America. They established numerous Welsh communities in their new homeland and assimilation was rapid, consequently there was a tendency to secularise and to lose the Welsh language. It was argued that this in turn resulted in the loss of those non-conformist values which contributed to upward social mobility. As a result community leaders both in North America and Wales came to feel that it would be advantageous to channel the existing emigration to a location where the degree of political autonomy could be achieved and where the threat of assimilation could be minimised. By 1860 it was generally agreed that Patagonia was an ideal location for such a venture.

Terms were negotiated with the Argentine government who were eager to consolidate their claim on that part of their territory and the initial group of settlers arrived in Patagonia during the winter of 1865. They located themselves in the Lower Chubut Valley where they experienced numerous difficulties in organising their economic activities, relying mainly on trade with the indigenous Tehuelche and the support of the Argentine authorities. It was 1873 before they were able to organise their economy to the point where more immigrants were able to join them. Subsequent immigration followed a pattern of arrival and period of adaptation during which time the new labour force could be employed to expand the infrastructure and thereby make way for a new group of immigrants. By the middle of the 1880's all the agricultural land in the Lower Chubut Valley had been claimed and a second settlement, named Cwm Hyfryd, was established in the Andes 400 miles to the west of the Lower Chubut Valley. Immigration ceased in 1914 by which time approximately 3,000 Welsh immigrants had entered the two settlements. Their descendants number approximately 10,000 today.

During the first fifty years of the settlements' existence there were several points of conflict with the Argentine authorities involving different conceptions of the political autonomy of the settlement. The Welsh settlers aimed to control local administration through their numerical superiority whereas the local officials found that this often conflicted with what they regarded as national interests. There was also conflict over the role of the Welsh language in education with the national officials denying the need for such a role and the settlers were obliged to finance their own schools. The conflict reached a peak at the turn of the century when some of the settlers sought the help of the British government in order to secede from the Argentine. Although the disagreement was resolved it prompted the Argentine authorities to stimulate non-Welsh migration to the area and also to remove the Welsh school teachers to remote parts of the Chubut territory.

The economic development focused upon agriculture which was organised through a co-operative society of which all the individual farmers were members. This society was responsible for marketing the produce and also extended credit facilities to the individual farmer. By 1914 there were seventeen branches in Patagonia and it dominated the regional economy but the international depression together with a series of poor harvests resulted in its liquidation in 1930. Thereafter the costs of agriculture increased whereas market prices were reduced. Yet the Welsh remained a group of relatively high status because of their control of agricultural land, although a number of non-Welsh farmers with considerable capital resources purchased land during the 1930's and 1940's at a time when capital was missing among the Welsh. This was the basis for an ethnic division of land use: the Welsh emphasised low risk extensive practices and the non-Welsh intensive, high-risk agriculture. The social and cultural life of the Welsh focused upon the seventeen non-conformist Chapels, which continued teaching the Welsh language.

Major changes have occurred since 1958 when Chubut achieved provincial status. In order to stimulate its industrial development, taxation advantages were granted and the economy underwent a profound structural change. Enterprises from the Buenos Aires metropolis moved in to take advantage of the incentives afforded the industrial sector but with investment which was not available locally. This development had had profound repercussions on the agricultural sector still dominated by the descendants of the Welsh settlers. The scarcity of labour in this sparsely populated area means that there is competition between industry and agriculture for existing labour with farmers unable to compete and where the marginal farmer may have to forget his petit-bourgeois status and enter the general labour force. This in turn has generated a greater tendency for reciprocal labour to be used, especially among Welsh farmers whose extensive agriculture involves uneven seasonal labour use. Thus marginalised, the agricultural sector is now coming into competition with the more strategically located and better financed agriculture of the Rio Negro.

While a high degree of agricultural reciprocity sustains the ethnic social networks, cultural assimilation has been rapid. The Chapels had been the focus of the community's medical insurance with collections being made among the congregation for needy families and all of the Chapels subscribed to medical insurance with the British Hospital in Buenos Aires. The creation of state-sponsored medical insurance for the self-employed by the Peron regime eliminated the need for such insurance and Chapel membership rapidly dropped off. Since the Chapel had been the only institution which fostered the Welsh language, following the Argentine government's elimination of the teaching of Welsh in the schools at the turn of the century, this had a marked effect upon language maintenance. More important was the elimination of those institutions such as the co-operative society, the irrigation society and the railway company which demanded a knowledge of Welsh as a job qualification. Their disappearance meant that there was little economic relevance for the language. With the decline of the agricultural sector in the overall economy there was a tendency to associate Welshness with a low socio-economic status so that the Welsh language became a marker of that status and there developed a tendency for the younger generation to reject the language and to identify with the wider society.

Discrimination against the Welsh community as an ethnic group, rather than as members of a social class or political affiliation cutting across ethnicity, is minimal. While their ethnic status has declined locally relative to other groups, they are not as low as others, such as the Chileans. Some compensate by drawing upon a British status which, to most Argentinians, is commensurate with being English, with a high ethnic status in the country. The Welsh are at a relative disadvantage however, in that members of the group have relatively little control over the means of production outside the agricultural sector. The majority of the Welsh descendants have identified with the Argentinian nation and do not seek any self-identity which contradicts the objectives and policies of the national authorities. Since they no longer constitute a threat to the political and cultural order, token support is extended for some of their activities with the celebration of the day of landing (*Gwyl y Glaniad*) having become a regional affair, as has the annual Eisteddfod (folk festival). The main dissatisfaction pertains to their inability to give children Welsh names, parents having to select from an official list of Christian names. This of course does not mean that individual Welsh have not been subject to the restriction of rights which have been applied by various regimes in recent years. Indeed some have been persecuted for their political views while others have lost their positions in public employment as a result of their views.

Glyn Williams

BIBLIOGRAPHY

Williams, Glyn, *The Desert and the Dream: A History of the Welsh Colonisation of Patagonia, 1865–1915,* University of Wales Press, Cardiff, 1975

— Cwm Hyfryd: A Welsh Settlement in the Patagonian Andes, *Welsh History Review,* Vol 9, No 1, 1978

— La Emigracion Galesa en la Patagonia 1865–1915, *Jahrbuch fur Geschichte von Staat Wirtschaft und Gesellschaft Lateinamerikas,* Vol 13, 1976

— The Structure and Process of Welsh Emigration to Patagonia, *Welsh History Review,* Vol 8, No 1, 1976

— Industrialisation and Ethnic Change in the Lower Chubut Valley, Argentina, *American Ethnologist,* Vol 5, No 3, 1978

— Differential Risk Strategies as Cultural Style among farmers in the Lower Chubut Valley, Patagonia, *American Ethnologist,* Vol 4, No 1, 1977

— Welsh Settlers and Native Americans, *Journal of Latin American Studies,* in Press

— *The Welsh in Patagonia: A Critical Bibliographic Review,* University of Wales Press, Cardiff, in Press

Williams, R. Bryn, *Y Wladfa,* University of Wales Press, Cardiff, 1962

REPORTS PUBLISHED BY THE MINORITY RIGHTS GROUP:

1 Religious minorities in the Soviet Union (Revised 1977 edition)
2 The two Irelands: the double minority — a study of inter-group tensions (Revised 1979 edition)
3 Japan's minorities: Burakumin, Koreans and Ainu (New 1974 edition) (30p)
4 The Asian minorities of East and Central Africa (up to 1971)
5 Eritrea and the Southern Sudan: aspects of wider African problems (New 1976 edition) (45p)
6 The Crimean Tartars, Volga Germans and Meskhetians: Soviet treatment of some national minorities (Revised 1980 edition)
7 The position of Blacks in Brazilian and Cuban Society (New 1979 edition)
8 Inequalities in Zimbabwe (New 1979 edition)
9 The Basques and Catalans (New 1977 edition) (tambien en castellano) ('The Basques' aussi en Francois auch auf deutsch)
10 The Chinese in Indonesia, the Philippines and Malaysia (45p)
11 The Biharis in Bangladesh (Revised 1977 edition)
12 Israel's Oriental Immigrants and Druzes (45p)
13 East Indians of Trinidad and Guyana (Revised 1980 edition)
14 The Rom: The Gypsies of Europe (Revised 1980 edition) (aussi en francais) (also in Romani)
15 What future for the Amerindians of South America? (Revised 1977 edition) (aussi en francais)
16 The new position of East Africa's Asians (Revised 1978 edition)
17 India and the Nagas (Revised 1980 edition)
18 The Montagnards of South Vietnam (45p)
19 The Namibians of South-West Africa (New 1978 edition)
20 Selective genocide in Burundi (aussi en francais)
21 Canada's Indians (Revised 1977 edition)
22 Race and Law in Britain and the United States (New 1979 edition)
23 The Kurds (Revised 1977 edition)
24 The Palestinians (Revised 1979 edition)
25 The Tamils of Sri Lanka (Revised 1979 edition)

Index